Fallen HERO

DON DAVIS

ST. MARTIN'S PAPERBACKS

For Ken Englade

Acknowledgments

Special thanks go once again to my California network of Jill and Sean in San Francisco, Cynthia in Los Angeles and Valerie in San Diego for their usual deadline assistance and support. As always, thanks to my wife Robin, my writing partner, primary researcher and editor. For their support, thanks to my agent, Mark Joly, and my editor, Charles Spicer. Warm thanks also to everyone at St. Martin's Paperbacks who worked on this book with speed, accuracy and enthusiasm.

Contents

1   Murder   *1*

2   Potrero Hill   *8*

3   College   *25*

4   The Pros   *44*

5   Da Bills   *55*

6   Cameras   *76*

7   Nicole   *95*

8   Abuse   *110*

9   Ron and A.C.   *122*

10   Monday, June 13   *134*

11   Tuesday, June 14   *151*

12   Wednesday, June 15   *160*

13   Thursday, June 16   *172*

Contents

14   Friday, June 17   *187*

15   O.J.'s Last Run   *204*

Epilogue   *219*

Appendix

I   Transcripts of Two 911 Calls Made by Nicole Simpson to Police on October 25, 1993   *239*

II   O.J. Simpson's Professional Career Record   *249*

III   Major Football Achievements   *250*

IV   Domestic Violence Hotlines and Shelters   *251*

1

MURDER

Crime is no stranger to Los Angeles. On any given day, the sprawling city coughs up an astonishing number of violations of the law, everything from traffic infractions on the car-choked freeways to murders as foul as the imagination can conceive. Still, such things are usually thought to be confined to neighborhoods that are not drenched in the kind of money that can buy security systems, electric gates, private guards, and bright lights. Not in communities such as Brentwood, an upscale community tucked between Beverly Hills and Bel Air, and not a hotbed of criminal activity. But then neither was Beverly Hills, where a wealthy couple named Kitty and Jose Menendez had been brutally slaughtered by their own two sons.

Erik and Lyle's circuslike trial seemed like ancient history on the night of Sunday, June 12, 1994. The hackneyed concept of "That Sort of Thing Could Never Happen Here" was about to have another hole punched in it, as the sun set in beautiful Brentwood on a day that had been wickedly hot throughout the country.

Sunday, June 12, nine days before the first day of summer, was one of those mild Southern California days when the high and low temperatures hover in the sixty-to-seventy-degree range. It was a good day to be outside doing something.

Shortly after the busy dinner hour that evening, the telephone rang at a neighborhood trattoria called Mezzaluna, a cream-colored restaurant with awnings on San Vicente Boulevard, a major avenue in Brentwood, that runs past the country club and is divided by a broad carpet of grassy mall.

Nicole Simpson was on the line. She had been in for dinner with seven other people, but in the confusion of leaving, she had forgotten her sunglasses. They were not an ordinary set of shades, but prescription ground, and she would need them the next day. Someone had turned them in already? Great, she said.

The tall, beautiful woman was a steady

customer at the trendy restaurant and had been pampered by the usual excellent treatment that evening for the two hours she was there. The reservations book listed her at the top of the list: Nicole (inside), her telephone number, a party of ten at 6:30 P.M. Only eight showed up, but since some of them were kids, things were pretty rambunctious. The group did not include her famous ex-husband, the football and media star O.J. Simpson, also a Brentwood resident. The divorced couple had attended a dance recital in which their daughter Sydney had performed at the Paul Revere Middle School, about midway between their two homes, on Sunday afternoon, but had parted when it was over.

Ron Goldman, a 6-foot-2 waiter with a handsome face and the carefully tended physique of someone who was both a model and bodybuilder, was a friend of Nicole's. He had been on duty at the restaurant that night, signing in at 4:30 P.M., but had not served her table. He was about to get off work and since he lived a short distance away, he volunteered to drop off the sunglasses as he walked back to his own apartment. Nicole's place was only four blocks from the restaurant. He stuck his time card into the clock and punched out at exactly

9:33 P.M. It was dark outside, with a finger-nail of moon showing in the night sky ever since the sun had gone down an hour and a half earlier.

Soon, he turned left off of San Vicente onto quiet South Bundy Drive, turned right beside the huge palm tree along the red curb and was on the narrow walkway of square Spanish tiles that led to the luxurious $650,000 Mediterranean-style condomin-ium that loomed above him like a castle in the L.A. night. It was walled and gated, but through a window near the red tile roofline, he could see that lights were still on inside. Nicole was expecting him.

The walkway was only five tiles wide, and his knees and elbows were brushed by showy clumps of lavender and white lilies of the Nile, and lacy Australian ferns that dipped toward him on the right. Over six feet tall, he had to duck to avoid the glossy fingerlike leaves of the tropical schefflera that hung overhead. Two palm trees were planted away from the gateway, atop a slope that was exploding in pink and white ground cover.

It was very dark beside the gate. Several small Malibu lights along the walkway were mostly covered by the bushes of lilies, a little light seeped out from inside the com-

4

pound around the edge of the gate, and a sodium-vapor streetlight turned the sidewalk a shade of dim orange. For someone less confident in himself than Ron, the little cul-de-sac could have been downright spooky. At the edge of the walk was a warning to anyone thinking of mischief: WESTEC SECURITY ARMED RESPONSE.

There was a mailbox to his left, and a call box from which he let Nicole know that he was there, bearing the requested sunglasses. This time of night, he thought, the kids, aged 9 and 5, were probably already asleep. Nicole buzzed the lock open.

The was a double set of gates, a tall one with an arched top made of heavy metal screen and covered with sanded wood on the inside for aesthetic purposes. It opened outward, to the right of a visitor. Just beyond it was an inner portal of ornate iron that opened to the left, almost bumping the mailbox.

Ron, tired from his own long day at work, went through the gates, skipped up the four steep steps, and hurried along the walkway that led alongside the townhouse to Nicole's front door. Tired or not, he perked up at the sight of his friend, always awed by the beauty of the elegant woman who was ten years older than him. The time was about

9:45, less than fifteen minutes since he had left Mezzaluna.

Shortly before 11 P.M., neighbors in the normally quiet and placid urban enclave heard an eruption of dogs barking madly. But there were no screams, no shouts of anger, no sounds of struggle, and everyone ignored the cries of the animals. Could have been a cat they were after, or maybe the dogs were just fighting among themselves.

Midnight passed quietly. But at 12:10 A.M. on Monday morning, a passerby happened to look toward the dark, narrow corridor that led to Nicole Simpson's town house. Both the inner and outer gates hung open. Nicole lay crumpled on her side in the alcove at the foot of the stairs, her face badly bruised and her throat slashed so deeply that her head was almost severed. According to a news magazine, she wore only a nightgown. The body of Ron Goldman was sprawled close by in the bushes, barefoot and with 22 stab wounds, his throat also slashed, obviously having fought violently against the attacker.

No weapon was visible, but a river of blood, black in the night, spread over the lower stairs and spilled halfway down the walkway toward the street. Nicole's large white dog, a Japanese Akita, his leash dragging behind him, stood near the bodies, a trail of bloody pawprints showing the path he had wandered near the bodies, almost as if guarding them, while waiting for someone to find his dead mistress and her friend. It looked like a butcher shop in paradise. A 911 emergency call quickly brought fleets of police cars roaring to the scene.

A mysterious tragedy of classic proportion, a story that would dominate the attention of the nation and send ripples of shock around the world, was just about to explode.

2

POTRERO HILL

The most famous professional football player of his generation, a powerful running back who held almost every important record there was for toting a football, was in San Francisco, unwinding after a rugged Sunday game against the 49ers at Kezar Stadium, when he ambled into an ice cream store with nothing more on his mind than the bruises he had accumulated that day, an occupational hazard in his line of work. He was a big man, but possessed with the smooth grace of a stalking tiger, even when doing nothing more than walking through a door. The muscles that powered him around, over or through huge pro football tacklers seemed almost ready to burst through the dark skin, and the careful eyes saw more than most mortals viewed, providing him with exceptional vision when dodging opponents bent on doing him harm. He had money, health, and reputation and had read his name in the newspapers so many times that he didn't need any proof that he was somebody special.

But like the gunfighters of the Old West, there was always some punk that seemed intent on standing in the way, ready to throw down a challenge, wanting to make his reputation by testing the best there ever was. In the ice cream store that Sunday afternoon was a group of lanky boys, members of a gang called the Superiors, talking trash and measuring themselves with teenage bravado. The football player was not impressed. He had seen too many ghetto kids like this, most of them already on the road from nowhere to nowhere, and their ragging of him, the Star of the Enemy Team, was not personal. Just jive. He ignored them.

One, however, wouldn't give it up. He was not in awe, and moved closer, standing out from his fellows as if disassociating himself from the mob, ready to prove himself. The kid looked up at the man. A tree! Hands like grappling hooks and a neck and shoulders that could pull a covered wagon over the

Rockies. The running back, if he cared to, would have been able to crush the boy like a bug. In the days before guns became the coin of the ghetto realm, making a reputation took more guts. Pulling a trigger on a defenseless victim is one thing, but challenging, *mano a mano* and without a weapon, the toughest dude in the National Football League, was something entirely different.

The kid didn't care. He was having fun and, anyway, he not only knew to whom he was talking but he also envied him with every fiber in his stripling body. He looked at his pals, and at the running back. "You ain't so tough. I'm going to break all your records, suckah!" he jeered. The running back didn't bother to even answer. Yeah. Right. Gang bait. He smiled at the kid's moxie, then left the store.

O.J. Simpson spun around and collected congratulations and high fives from his chums in the Superiors, as Jim Brown walked away, eating his ice cream, the incident already forgotten.

The most famous professional baseball player of his generation, a center fielder whose fame was underlined by the magic in his glove and the pop in his Hillerich &

Bradsby bat, was in San Francisco, unwinding on a day off from the rigors of trying to play decent baseball in Candlestick Park, where the tornado-like swirling winds made an adventure out of even a routine fly ball. He was a big man, possessed of the moves that God bestows on few mortals, who combined blinding speed with pure power, but his muscles were not of the bulging variety. Instead, he was almost sleek, with an economy of movement, a cheetah ready to dash away and bring down his prey.

Major league pitchers feared him and batters cursed the way he casually chased down fly balls for outs when ordinary fielders probably would not even have been in the baseball's same zip code. His plays and reputation had been made over the years, through hard work and accomplishment, and one particular play, an over-the-head catch at the warning track while running full tilt with his back to the ball, in the World Series, no less, would forever be on highlight films. He did not have to prove anything.

But he had heard of a kid who was in trouble, a fine little athlete already walking the short plank that a ghetto provides for those who want to choose shortcuts over hard work. So the ballplayer made time on one of his rare off days when he would have been working with troubled kids at the Booker T. Washington Center, and now was standing in the tiny living room of a small apartment in the Potrero Hill section of San Francisco, while the boy's mama yelled upstairs for the kid to come down. The youngster had just returned that Monday morning from a stint in Juvenile Hall, this time having spent a whole weekend there for swiping a keg of beer for a gang party, and he was expecting another swatting.

Instead, when the morose kid came down the stairs, he discovered that his hero was sitting there, waiting for him like a pal from his gang of the moment—the Persian Warriors—might have done. Cockiness faded immediately in the light of greatness, and the famous ballplayer asked, "You want to come out with me this afternoon?"

With clearance from Mama, young O.J. Simpson walked out the front door, side by side with Willie Mays, and spent the rest of his day learning about being something more than a tough guy. The Superstar didn't bother showing his press clippings or strutting around the neighborhood. Instead Mays took the young Persian Warrior, who liked to spend many afternoons stealing anything from a pie to a slab of beef, to places like the dry cleaners and another store to do errands. Then the two stopped by the home of a friend of Mays to help plan a banquet. Finally the sports hero brought the young man to his own home to spend some time. Ordinary stuff. Willie Mays didn't need a gang.

"I had an entirely different outlook on everything after that day with Willie Mays," Simpson would recall two decades later for a *Sports Illustrated* writer. "I can't really say that it turned my life around, just like that. I honestly believe that I would have made it on my own. But that time with Mays made me realize that my dream was possible. Willie wasn't superhuman. He was an ordinary person, so there was a chance for me."

Mays wasn't quite through with the boy. He came and fetched O.J. from a dance one evening for another session of just hanging out together, when he told the boy that, yes, he was a great athlete, but that O.J. had the potential to be even greater. He had to try! Mays did not know that he was launching a superstar. The ballplayer was only trying to make a positive difference in the life of a kid on the edge. He wanted to let the boy know that the hard path to athletic success was far different than the easy one that would end in prison, drug addiction, or helpless frustration.

Simpson began to focus on his books and his future.

If you handed Orenthal James Simpson a lemon, he is not the type of person who would use it to make lemonade. Instead of perhaps establishing a nickel-a-glass lemonade stand, he would turn the lemon into a multimillion-dollar business, sell franchises, go on television to advertise it, and watch his bank account grow even larger, smiling all the time, as if such a transformation was the easiest thing in the world.

Make no mistake of it. Life indeed handed young Simpson a whole sack of lemons, and the scenario outlined above is exactly how he handled the situation, for he simply refused to allow anything or anybody to defeat him. "Every time in my life there has been a negative, I've been able to turn it into a positive," he told author Dave Newhouse, who interviewed him for the book *Heisman: After the Glory.* "I grew up in what people would look at and think wasn't a good situation—the Potrero Hill district of San Francisco. I lived in the projects, in a building with eight other families. But we were like one big family. I thought Potrero Hill was the greatest place in the world. There was always a park to play in, always someone's house to go to if you needed something. I grew up in a lot of love."

He was born, a fat little baby, in San Francisco's Stanford University Hospital on July 9, 1947, the same year that Jackie Robinson signed with the Brooklyn Dodgers to break the color line in major league baseball. Negro ballplayers were nonexistent in major league sports of the time, but in about two decades, the little son of Eunice Durton Simpson and Jimmie Simpson would set new standards for athletes of all colors.

From the beginning, there were obstacles to overcome. He suffered from a calcium deficiency that doctors said might be rickets, and someone watching him struggling to learn how to walk, laden with braces to strengthen his bones, could well wonder whether the child would even be able to put one foot in front of another, much less become a football player of heroic proportion.

In addition to other problems, he had been given the very, very strange name of Orenthal by an aunt who had given her own children common names like Stanley and Pam. Years later, Simpson would ponder

15

the question of his name. "Lord knows where she got that Orenthal," he said. "She must have been sick once, and it just came up." That it would need nickname was a certainty, but no one could tell that it would become recognized around the world.

Another lemon was put into O.J.'s bag when he was five years old. His father, a custodian at the Federal Reserve Bank, left the family. Living in bleak, low-income government housing on Potrero Hill with his mother, brother Leon and sisters Shirley and Carmelita, separated from his father, the young Orenthal seemed to possess most of the reasons for going bad. And as he grew up in the rough neighborhoods in the City by the Bay, he certainly took quite a few walks on the wild side. "I was somebody who didn't care about anything, and the best thing you can say about me and trouble was that I was borderline," he would later tell a newspaper interviewer.

School books would prove to hold little fascination for him, and discipline was not his highest priority in life. Five times his rebellious free spirit won him suspensions from school, although with a personality that wouldn't quit, it was hard for the teachers to stay mad at him.

His joining up with the Superiors led to a

series of infractions, as the tough guys set out to prove themselves and wound up visiting Juvenile Hall. Even today, O.J. classifies the youthful fights and other problems as the product of aggressiveness, not the sign of a kid going bad.

But the schools did offer something that he liked—in fact, something that he loved. Sports. As a little kid, he had begun playing Little League baseball as a catcher, imitating Willie Mays even to the point of wearing his hat so that it would fall off when he ran the bases, just like Willie's did.

At Galileo High in the mid-1960s, O.J. found a second home on the playing fields. He ran track. He played baseball. And he learned how to be part of a team and carry a football.

Growing up in California, even the fog-soaked Bay Area, gives youngsters with athletic talent a way to blow off steam and develop their skills in ways other than taking dope and participating in violent acts. *Time* magazine termed the state a "Hot House of Champions" because of its seemingly endless conveyor belt that regularly dumps off a new load of winners. Thirty-two percent of the medals won by the United States in the 1988 Summer Olympics were won by people who were from

California or who had lived there. "It was just natural that we played sports anywhere, anytime," O.J. noted.

So in the nearby public sports park's fields and gymnasium, Simpson found a purpose. "For the gangs of those days, the rec center was the focus of activity. There was always room, and there were always opportunities," he said. Sports would become his ticket out of the ghetto. The crowd he hung out with also dodged the deadly bullets of drugs, because they all wanted to be athletes, which meant they had to get their rest and keep their bodies in top shape. You could be a jock or a junkie, but not both. "I couldn't sing and dance, and I wasn't going to be a brain surgeon, so it had to be sports."

At Galileo High, O.J. Simpson showed up for his first practice looking like a giant. At 5-foot-10, weighing 160 pounds, he was literally head and shoulders above most of the other members of the team, because Galileo, located at the edge of Chinatown, had an enrollment that was seventy percent Asian. The coach took a look at the big guy and saw a lineman, somebody who could put that bulk to use clearing a path for some fleet little halfback. One day at practice, Coach Jack McBride became the first adult involved in organized athletics to see O.J. Simpson run with a football tucked beneath his arm. The fluid grace, the deceptive speed, the churning legs were on display only a short time before McBride said Simpson's days as a tackle on the line were over. He was assigned to duty in the backfield. O.J. would later laugh at the experience. "We had an Asian guy, tough as nails. But he was only 5-foot-5 and weighed 120 pounds, and he was my offensive guard!"

The decision paid off handsomely. When Galileo went to face off against mighty St. Ignatius High School, St. Ignatius had won nineteen games in a row. Galileo had lost nineteen of the last twenty-three it had played. St. Ignatius had momentum, strength, and reputation. Galileo had O.J. Simpson. Trailing in the third quarter by a score of 25–10, the St. Ignatius quarterback threw a pass, and O.J., playing cornerback on defense, picked it out of the arms of the player who caught it. Ninety yards. Touchdown. Later Simpson, running out of the backfield, caught a screen pass. Eighty yards. Touchdown. Finally, he caught a swing pass. Sixty yards. Touchdown. Galileo won, 31–25.

There were still lessons to be learned off the field, however, about the projects and life and the future. Another of his former high school coaches, Jack McCaffrey, described O.J. as being streetwise enough to know that "if he elected to go down and act like the rest of the idiots, he wasn't going to get anywhere." His intelligence began to show up in peculiar ways, not in the traditional manner of getting good grades in class, but out on the streets, where he was popular in almost every crowd. "There were guys who could have taken O.J. in a fight, but he had a way of manipulating people, of making them like him," said one friend. It was an early indicator of the poise and leadership that would propel O.J. throughout his life.

And Simpson's football career was almost nipped in the bud. He and a couple of buddies opted one day to skip class in favor of something that provided a little bit more fun, shooting dice in the school bathroom. But Coach McBride happened by and found them and was faced with a crisis. Here was his star player violating school rules. Many coaches would have let it slide, but McBride played it exactly right and trotted the three miscreants off to see the principal.

McBride told the principal what had happened and handed over the pair of offending dice, then walked out the door, probably thinking about who the heck could replace Simpson as halfback. He knew that O.J. was quick with a football, but was about to learn that the kid had a brain on him, too. The dean told O.J. to close the office door and Simpson walked out of the room, shutting it behind him. Wait a minute, called the principal, where are you going? Simpson explained that he wasn't shooting craps at all, and the coach had just asked him to bring the other two guys to the office. Fine, said the principal. Good-bye. Then the principal suspended Al Cowlings and Joe Bell, both of whom thought their friend was pretty nifty for being able to cough up such an excuse under pressure.

"I really wasn't interested in studying or going on with school," O.J. once recalled. "But Mr. McBride told me, 'You'll get nowhere letting people give you stuff. You've got to work for everything.' I never forgot that."

Simpson went on to be named to San Francisco's All-City Team, and in his senior year, he led the city in scoring. But Galileo just didn't have the horses to back him up in its weak program. The team was winless in nine games his junior year of playing, and compiled only a mediocre record of five wins and four losses in his final year. That was the only winning season that O.J. enjoyed in high school. The disappointing football program at the little high school and the bad grades of the promising athlete did not lure scouts from university football programs, who would have had to go out of their way to check out the high-scoring kid at Galileo.

Something else was at work on O.J. Simpson during that period of his life. Despite the bag of lemons, which now included being the best unknown athlete in San Francisco, positive things were settling him down on the personal front. Although his father had not lived with the family since O.J. was a tyke, he still lived nearby, and if Eunice was having problems disciplining her lanky son, she would call on Jimmie Simpson, who would hurry over, belt in hand, to dish out a little attitude adjustment for the growing boy. Jimmie's life was also going through a change at the time. He gave up custodial work to learn how to cook professionally, becoming a cook in the cafeteria of the bank where he once swept floors. And Eunice provided as much inspiration as a mother possibly could, never complaining about her own job.

For twenty-seven years, she worked the midnight shift at San Francisco General

Hospital's psychiatric ward. Part of her job was to accompany released patients back home in other states, and her awed co-workers called her the "Flying Nun." She would sometimes return home battered and bruised from dealing with a violent psychiatric patient. The divorced parents made certain, however, that the family remained a family, and regularly spent the holidays together. If the rebellious young O.J. wanted a cop out excuse for failure, he would have had to look beyond his own doorstep.

Even beyond that doorstep was a world of discipline in the projects, where strong-willed mothers ruled with iron hands, automatically watching over each other's kids. "If Mrs. Simpson saw me doing something wrong, she'd slap me quick," said O.J.'s boyhood pal Joe Bell. "And if my mother saw O.J. doing something wrong, she'd slap him. Neighbors looked after their neighbors' kids."

There was another attraction for O.J. at Galileo. Before he graduated in 1965, he fell in love with beautiful fellow student Marguerite Whitley, who had been dating another football player. But she and big Al Cowlings had an argument and Al sent his closest buddy, O.J., over to make amends. Cowlings, having apparently forgotten the

23

lesson of the crap game, eventually realized that he had made a big mistake. O.J. always seemed to come out of these episodes a winner, and Cowlings lost his girlfriend to his pal. He would needle O.J. about such moments years later, even when they became teammates on the Buffalo Bills.

The direction from home, the sweetheart, the success in sports, and the fateful meeting with Willie Mays when O.J. was only fourteen years old in 1961 all were creating a potent stew that would turn out an extraordinary adult.

Years later, after he was inducted into the Hall of Fame, Eunice Simpson told reporters that O.J. had predicted greatness for himself from an early age. "He had always said, 'One of these days you're going to read about me.' And my oldest daughter would always say, 'In the police report.'"

3

COLLEGE

On Phelan Avenue in San Francisco sat an institution that offered a lot of things that were pleasing to the new high school graduate. The City College of San Francisco, founded in 1935 as part of California's extraordinary community college system, was located in O.J.'s hometown, tuition was free to state residents, and it offered not only a two-year degree but also sixteen sports. On its fifty-six-acre suburban campus, O.J. Simpson would open the door to the exciting new world that loomed beyond Potrero Hill.

Once again, the coaches misread the situation. They had a halfback returning to the City College team who was an excellent runner and had earned the starting job. Simpson went into his first college game as a defensive back and third-string running back, something that the gods of football, who apparently knew what destiny had in store, could not tolerate. The star halfback was injured, then the second-stringer and the coaches were left with no choice but to put Simpson in the backfield to start the next game.

O.J. recalled years later that three games later, he felt that every college in the United States was suddenly on his doorstep. That was not far from fact, because after his first season, scholarship offers poured in from fifty colleges.

The record he stacked up on the playing field for those two seasons at City College are astonishing, even today, after so many other great athletes have set impressive marks of their own. Simpson was a Junior College All-American for both years, led his team to an overall mark of seventeen wins, only two losses and one tie, and appearances in two Prune Bowl post-season games.

He wrote new national junior college records by rushing for 2,445 yards—almost 10 yards every time he carried the ball—and scoring 50 touchdowns. And that was just in his first season.

Several schools almost scooped him up

after his freshman season, including Arizona State and Utah. But a radio broadcast that O.J. had heard a few years earlier changed Simpson's life.

As a kid living in the San Francisco projects, he had not paid much attention to big-time college football. He idolized the 49ers, and although quarterback John Brodie was out with a broken arm in the 1963 season, O.J. and his buddies still enjoyed sneaking into end-zone stands at Kezar Stadium, and after the game, they went down to the field to see the famous players up close. Pro football. That was where it was at. The 'Niners might struggle, but at least you could see the big stars from other teams. From 1957 through 1965, Simpson never missed a San Francisco 49ers home game.

But on New Year's Day of 1963, the radio was broadcasting a game from elsewhere, and O.J. listened in fascination.

There was a team called the University of Southern California playing in something called the Rose Bowl. He had never heard of either of them. USC, the announcer said, was playing for the national championship and its big gun was Willie Brown, the star halfback. Willie Brown was black, just like O.J., and the boy listened intently to Brown's progress. He heard the cheers, the spirit, the description of Tommy Trojan riding a horse on the field after a USC score, and he liked what he heard. At the age of fifteen, he decided he wanted to go to that school—that USC, wherever it was.

But USC was no City College with open admission, and O.J. didn't have the grades after high school to make the leap. And he still didn't have the grades after his freshman year at City College. Other colleges were making pitches and O.J. was wavering, until USC recruiter Marv Goux, who knew of Simpson's dream of wearing red and gold, set him down for a long talk, like a surrogate father. Stay in school at City College, Goux advised, at least through the fall semester. Play ball and work hard on your grades. It's all up to you. Do well enough and you can come to USC, Goux promised. O.J. remembered the radio broadcast again and decided to stay at City College for the fall semester. He had already developed the determination that he could get whatever he wanted. Nobody was going to stop him, not even himself.

City College was happy to have him back. He scored 54 touchdowns and ran for 310 yards in a single game, both new records.

Sure enough, USC beckoned. Others tried, but fell short, particularly after a recruiting trip to Los Angeles put the impressionable O.J. in the presence of Trojan running back Mike Garrett, winner of the Heisman Trophy, the symbol of the best college football player in America. Once again, he saw greatness up close. Other schools and athletes liked to show off, but Garrett was a regular guy who wore tennis shoes and drove a Chevy. Without knowing it, Garrett was playing Simpson's tune.

As a recruit, he was invited to the Rose Bowl game between USC and Purdue in 1966, which the Trojans lost. The locker room was deathly quiet as the players sat stunned, even weeping. Simpson, who had not even yet put on a Southern Cal uniform, wandered among them, saying, "Don't worry about this loss. We'll be back next year."

In the spring of 1967, O.J. Simpson enrolled at the University of Southern California. To pass the time until autumn and football, he decided to run track, and was put on the 440-yard relay team, which then immediately went out and set a world's record (38.6 seconds). The team won the NCAA track championship.

On June 24, 1967, O.J. married his high school sweetheart, Marguerite.

It was another world.

Where City College had been a choice of last resort, USC represented the attainment of a dream for O.J. Simpson. He was on a football scholarship, so he didn't have to worry about the high tuition and room-and-board charges that most students faced, but O.J. and Marguerite may have felt like aliens from another planet when they arrived at the campus in the middle of Los Angeles.

They were not rich, and USC at the time was a school for the white offspring of wealthy parents. Minorities were really in the minority, and only six percent of the students were African-Americans. For most students, black people were residents of the nearby Watts ghetto, not the sort of people who would drive up in a fancy German automobile to one of the Greek fraternity houses on Rich Row. To be smart, to be rich and to be good-looking, even if you had to work on your tan in Mexico, was the goal of a typical USC student. Drinking beer at the campus pub, Traditions, and going off campus for chili cheeseburgers at Tommy's were not bad ways to spend a day.

But, oh, they did like their gladiators. USC also had the reputation of being a jock school, a football team with a few classrooms thrown in for good measure. The school had more NCAA championships than any other university, and every Summer Olympics since 1912 had seen at least one USC athlete carry off a gold medal. And in the middle of the campus stands the statue of Tommy Trojan, the symbolic Roman soldier who salutes the victories of the USC Trojans.

O.J. came to the campus unknown to those who had not heard about the whiz kid from San Francisco who could run one hundred yards in 9.3 seconds. But at 6-foot-1, 205 pounds, and in perfect physical condition, Simpson was about to step into the starring role in football's glamour position as the running back at the University of Southern California.

And he had fallen into the hands of John McKay, a methodical West Virginian who had been head coach of the Trojans since 1960 and had ridden the wild roller coaster that is college football to both its highs and lows. He considered the football field to be a classroom, and did not want players around who could not think quickly and adapt to a new situation. What McKay saw in O.J. Simpson was a charming, outgoing kid with jackrabbit speed and the exceptional peripheral vision that allowed him to see the entire field at a glance. He knew O.J. had a gallon of potential, but was about a quart low in fundamentals. The teachings of high school and junior college had not fully prepared him for the bigger and stronger arenas in which he would be playing in Division I college football. Every time O.J. would fumble the ball or take a misstep in a practice, McKay would patiently try to make him do better the next time.

McKay was no stranger to handling star jocks. Willie Brown had been an exceptional athlete, and he was followed by Mike Garrett, who only had finished playing for USC in 1965 and had won the Heisman Trophy. McKay congratulated them and looked for someone to continue the coach's experiment, running a tailback out of an "eye" formation. In Simpson, he got just what he needed, a bigger and faster model, the latest evolution in the Brown-Garrett mold, a stud horse who could carry the ball dozens of times in a game and have wind left in reserve.

When critics said McKay made his famous tailback carry the ball too often, the coach would shrug and reply that it shouldn't be a problem because a football doesn't weigh very much.

The coach called Simpson "Jay" but soon

the tens of thousands of fans who would fill up the Rose Bowl stadium for a USC game would be screaming the tailback's nickname. O.J. had naturally lead to him being called "Orange Juice" instead of Orenthal James. But stadiums were soon rocking with a nickname that had spun off a nickname. "Juice!" they would cheer madly. "Juice! Juice! Juice!"

McKay wanted him to run, let him run, *made* him run, and O.J. responded by learning and improving almost with each step, getting past the slow start of the junior college level of coaching and setting sail for an All-American season. McKay knew that Jay, as a junior college transfer, had only two years of eligibility at USC. There was no time to waste.

In his premier game as a Trojan, O.J. caught a swing pass the first time he touched the ball and sprinted fifteen yards. He finished with 94 yards as the Trojans beat Washington State. He jacked it up a notch against Texas in the following seek, to 158 yards, then hit Michigan State for 190 yards and two touchdowns, and Stanford fell victim to the Trojans as Juice clocked 160 yards.

That was nice, and worthy of national

ranking, but Southern Cal then faced a major test, a wall of USC tears known as Notre Dame. Playing on Irish sod in South Bend, Indiana, the Trojans had not won since 1939. Football experts said that the Notre Dame game would prove whether the Trojans were real and if this kid Simpson was ready to play with the big boys. Notre Dame got off to a 7–0 lead, but then fumbled the ball and USC tied the game on a seven-play drive in which O.J. carried the ball six times, including diving in from the one-yard line for the touchdown. That was just the appetizer. Simpson finished the day with 38 carries for 150 yards and three touchdowns, USC won 24–7 and Tommy Trojan had knocked Touchdown Jesus for a loop.

The newspaper reporters flooded into the locker room after the game and O.J. learned something about himself as the tough and mumble East Coast writers accosted him, wanting some news about the kid from the Left Coast. Instead of a sulking young man or a tongue-tied jock or a cocky and conceited athlete, they discovered that O.J. Simpson was a personable and likable fellow with a quick smile and a ready reply to even inane questions. He enjoyed the verbal jousts, answered all their questions, shared a couple of laughs, and became their buddy.

O.J., for the rest of his life in sports, would enjoy an extraordinary rapport with the reporters who covered the games. He liked them and they liked him, and their stories and headlines and television bits showed it.

The season wasn't over. O.J. led Southern Cal to an astounding win over Washington, when he carried 30 times for 235 yards and two touchdowns, one of which was a patented, tackle-shedding 86-yard sprint. The next week, they also won at Oregon, but O.J. was sidelined by a foot injury that forced him to sit out the next game, a win over California.

Undefeated and ranked Number One in the nation, the Trojans stumbled badly in the mud after a week of rain in Corvallis, Oregon, and a surprisingly tough Oregon State team beat them 3–0, knocking USC from first place and allowing crosstown rival UCLA to grab the top spot in the polls. Juice logged 188 yards on 33 carries in the goo, but the loss tarnished the Trojan season. UCLA had suffered similarly against Oregon State, but managed a 16–16 tie and in the polls, a tie looks better than a loss.

That set up the game of the year in college football, as Number Two USC, with Juice back and healthy at tailback, squaring off against the Number One UCLA Bruins, led by sharpshooting quarterback Gary Beban. Everything in college football was at stake that Saturday, including the national championship and the Heisman, which was certain to go either to O.J. or to Beban.

Beban was hot that day, completing 16 out of 24 passes for 301 yards and two touchdowns. But O.J. was not to be denied. In one of the greatest runs of his career in the second quarter with the scored knotted at 7–7, he took the ball at the UCLA 13-yard line, knocked off one tackler, then shook loose of two more, and dodged a pair of diving Bruin defenders. As he closed on the goal, three UCLA defenders stood there waiting for him and O.J. tore through them as if they had only been there to direct traffic. Thirteen yards is a minuscule piece of real estate and he never changed direction while breaking through eight tackles to score the touchdown.

Later, in the fourth quarter with UCLA ahead by six points, Simpson was exhausted, thanks in part to a UCLA plan to end his habit of laying on the ground a few seconds after each run to catch his breath. Throughout the game, when O.J. was tackled, several blue shirts appeared beside him and friendly UCLA players helped him immediately to his feet. Simpson, worn out, told the quarterback not to give him the ball for a play so he could catch his breath. Right, said the quarterback, who promptly got to the line, changed the play and called out "twenty-three"—the signal for Simpson to run to the left. Exhausted and astonished, O.J. faked right and ran to the left, followed some good blocks, cut across the middle of the field, sliced past the pursuing defenders and made it into the end zone untouched all the way from the Trojan 36-yard line. He dropped the ball and kept running because he was too tired to stop. "That's the damnedest run I've ever seen," McKay whispered to himself on the sideline as the 64-yard touchdown scamper came to an end. Simpson finished the day with 30 rushes for 127 yards and gave the Trojans a 21–20 victory. "It was the greatest game I've played in because all the chips were on the table," Beban observed.

In the winner's locker room after the game, Beban shook the hand of Juice and said, "O.J., you're the best." Simpson returned the compliment. "Gary, you're the greatest. It's too bad one of us had to lose." Again, the young man was showing an ability to communicate, to be a nice guy and to manage an awkward situation, all traits that would follow him well into adulthood.

The Trojans beat Indiana in the Rose Bowl, allowing O.J. to redeem his promise to the losing Trojan team of 1966. They also won the national championship for 1967 and O.J., the kid from Potrero Hill, was named an All-American. He had run for 1,415 yards with 266 carries, leading the nation in both categories. He also threw three touchdown passes. United Press International voted Simpson Player of the Year.

Then came the Heisman voting at the Downtown Athletic Club in New York. Beban was given 1,968 points by the voters and O.J. Simpson, only a junior and playing his first major college season, received 1,722 points. "O.J. had a phenomenal year. I was honored for my career," said the modest Beban. Simpson remembered years later, speaking with equal sportsmanship, that he did not bear any ill will about the vote. "In my heart, I believe that Gary was just as valuable to his team in 1967 as I was to mine."

Some of that was smoke. Mike Garrett threw a party for the USC team after the Rose Bowl victory and O.J. spent a lot of time staring at Beban's Heisman, the bulky statue of an old-time football player, arm outstretched and legs churning as if dodging a tackle. He considered how close he had come to picking up the prize, and deter-mined that in his senior year, he would get one of those statues for himself.

When the 1968 season rolled around, O.J. Simpson was no longer a surprise to oppo-nents. Every football fan in America knew his name and coaches planned their entire games around how to stop him. To compli-cate matters, the Trojans only had fifteen starters from the 1967 championship team returning for the new season and it was the youngest team that McKay ever coached. Coming off the 1967 championship season, when things went so well, the new version of the Trojans would specialize in winning ugly, having to come from behind to win. In his autobiography, McKay stated that USC simply had no one other than Simpson who could carry the ball. "I knew that if he didn't do it, it wasn't going to get done. We planned to overpower people with a fantastic athlete and good blocking." The result was most of the USC games featured a herd of blockers leading Juice forward in one of two plays that McKay had designed for the situation—Student Body Right or Student Body Left.

O.J. inspired his teammates, told them they could do it, made them try, and they responded. At midseason they were Number One again and the magic of O.J. Simpson was still baffling opponents. After Coach Murray Warmath watched Juice pile up four touchdowns, catch six passes, run for 236 yards, a reporter asked him if he was aware that Simpson carried the ball 36 times in that game. Warmath shook his head wearily. "I thought it was 400 times," he replied.

The Trojans finished the year with a record of 9–1–1 with a loss in the Rose Bowl to unbeaten Ohio State.

Honors were falling all over O.J. Simpson as he wrapped up his collegiate career, and he was flying around the country to accept them, following a punishing schedule that kept him out of vital Rose Bowl practices and wore him out. Adding to the physical wear and tear was the distress of worrying about Marguerite, who was pregnant and about to give birth. "It just has to be a boy," Simpson said. His wife quickly added that if it were, the child would not be named Orenthal. Even the indefatigable Simpson finally admitted to Coach McKay that he was tired, out of juice. Still, he ran for 171 yards in the Rose Bowl game on 28 carries and six pass receptions.

He was voted an All-American again and

after an abbreviated major college career, he could hang up those spikes, having run for 3,295 yards and 34 touchdowns in 649 rushing attempts. His team, in the 22 games of his USC career, went 19–2–1 and he broke 19 school, conference, and NCAA records. UPI and the Associated Press voted him player of the year, *Sport* magazine named him man of the year. Nobody had ever done better in two years of collegiate football competition.

So he found himself back in New York, back at the Downtown Athletic Club, to become the thirty-fourth winner of the Heisman Memorial Trophy. In typical fashion, he won by the largest margin in the first half-century that the trophy had been handed out, receiving 855 of the possible 1,042 votes and a total of 2,853 points for first place. Leroy Keyes, the mighty running back of Purdue, was second with 1,103 points, and Notre Dame quarterback Terry Hanratty was third with 387 points. At the Heisman dinner that night, someone handed him a note that said back in Los Angeles, Marguerite had given birth to their first child, a daughter named Arnelle. It was a moment to reflect upon later, as an example of what was pulling O.J. and Marguerite apart so slowly that they were hardly able to discern the inevitable drift. He was on the road, playing ball and accepting awards, while she was home, separated not infrequently by the entire continent from her husband.

Something else was happening at that time that would be repeated often. Not even out of college, not even under contract to a pro team, O.J. was already looking over the horizon toward what he could do after the brief life of a football star had run its course. He decided to skip his final semester of USC and that nonsense that a college player who brings in millions of dollars in revenue for an institution cannot receive payment of any kind. O.J. and Marguerite and baby Arnelle were living on $125 a month. Since universities, which scoop up millions of dollars because of athletic teams, forbid payment to the athletes who perform, the most popular college football player of his day was barely getting by. Simpson decided the time had come to make some money on his popularity and ability. He did not obtain his degree in public administration, but, then, he didn't really need it. In quick succession, he signed a $250,000 three-year contract with Chevrolet, agreed to endorse Royal Crown Cola for three years at $120,000, and inked a deal with ABC-TV to join the broadcast teams at specific sports events at $6,000 per event. He became a celebrity! The kid from the San Francisco low-income government housing projects visited Sacramento and Governor Ronald Reagan asked for his autograph.

The poor days were history and O.J. would never let them return to haunt him or his family. Among the other things he said he learned at USC was which fork to pick up at a dinner table, and the other social graces he needed to mingle in white society. The success would bring a risk, because the handsome young football star was being deluged by the attention of beautiful women who climbed all over him, and he wasn't strong enough to ignore them. The result was putting strain on his marriage.

Coach McKay bade Jay a fond farewell and started looking for a new tailback, knowing that the one who was leaving this time could really never be replaced. The coach flatly predicted that O.J. Simpson was on his way to becoming the greatest runner that professional football had ever seen.

4

THE PROS

Near the end of the 1968–1969 professional football season, the Philadelphia Eagles fumbled away their future. The first choice in the annual draft of college players goes to the team with the worst record and the Eagles were sitting pretty in what was being called "The O.J. Simpson Sweepstakes" because they had lost eleven games in a row. Then they muffed it by beating Detroit and New Orleans on consecutive Sundays, being able to salvage a little pride with a record of two wins and twelve losses, but turning the top draft choice over to the Buffalo Bills. The Bills were truly dreadful, bumbling through the season with only one win and one tie in fourteen games. It was a case, however, of the loser getting to wear the biggest grin.

The draft began on January 28, 1969, and before it was done, some four hundred and forty-two players would be chosen by the sixteen teams of the National Football League and the ten teams in the American Football League. But all of the attention at the Belmont Plaza Hotel in New York was focused right at the top of the pyramid, right on O.J. Simpson.

Possible draftees at the time were rated by a complex system of scouting and tests known as BLESTO, the acronym for the teams that began it in 1963, the Bears-Lions-Eagles-Steelers Talent Organization. Scouts who had gone from school to school, attended spring practices, studied reports, and watched the season unfold combined their data so that everyone was evaluated on the same scale. The physical skills, the speed in the 40-yard dash, height and weight, statistics, and injuries were mixed in with such intangibles as a player's aggressiveness and character, and weighed on a scale ranging from 4.1 at the bottom to 0.0 at the top. There is no such thing as a perfect player, and few ever got below 1.0. The men gathered at the draft headquarters saw that O.J. graded out at an astonishing 0.4, clearly the athlete of the generation.

Questions lingered as the draft neared. Would the Bills take him? Would they trade him away for a bunch of talented players? What about O.J.'s desire to play in the NFL, since the Bills were in the AFL? How would a kid from California react to being told that his future lay in the frozen wastes of Buffalo winters? How much money would it take to bring Simpson under contract?

"I'd prefer to play for a California team, and I'd love to play in New York, although not to live there," said O.J., playing his cards carefully. "But I'll take it as it comes." Behind the scenes, there was word that Simpson and his agent, Chuck Barnes of Indianapolis, might file legal action to test the validity of the draft if he were chosen by the Bills. That probably was nothing more than a bargaining ploy, but it sent chills up a few spines in Buffalo.

Author A. S. "Doc" Young, in his book *Black Champions of the Gridiron*, reported that O.J. was awaiting the draft results in the home of his mother-in-law in San Francisco when Buffalo Bills owner Ralph C. Wilson telephoned at 6:30 A.M. California time to tell the USC running back that he had been chosen and the Bills were delighted to land him. O.J. replied that he was happy to be aboard. By the way, Simpson queried, how's the weather in Buffalo today? "Beautiful," oozed Wilson, ignoring the minor fact that the temperature was pegged at four degrees below zero.

The contract negotiations plodded on through most of 1969 as the Bills sought to come to terms with the player that the *New York Times* had crowned as "possibly the most prized collegian in pro football history." On August 9, the parties finally signed a four-year agreement and, much later, it leaked out that O.J. would be making $250,000. With his list of endorsements and other deals, including a $100,000 loan from the Bills, he began his professional life with an income of about $1 million.

Signed, sealed, and delivered, O.J. Simpson went off to play football in Buffalo, New York, and was soon wondering if hell had frozen over.

It was the same story all over again. He may have won the Heisman Trophy, stacked up more college records than any one individual had a right to do, and be slavishly sought by professional teams, but the one man he needed to impress apparently could not have cared less about the star player who walked into the pathetic herd of Buffalos. The team that had won exactly one game the previous season had as its coach John Rauch, and he was damned if he was going to change his ways just because a new rookie was in town.

"Not my style," declared Rauch when asked about how he was going to use Simpson's running ability. "I'm not going to build my offense around one back, no matter how good he is. It's too easy for the pros to set up defensive keys. O.J. can be a terrific pass receiver, and we expect him to block, too." Rauch had come to Buffalo after three years of coaching the fearsome Oakland Raiders and in his first year with the Bills had lost more games than in his full tenure at Oakland. Rauch believed in the pass, not the run, but Air Rauch crashed more often than not, and the offensive line wasn't good enough to protect a premier running back.

So in his first season as a professional O.J. was seen by his coach more as a pass receiver than a runner. Rauch figured the burning speed could best be harnessed if Simpson was out in the flat, as a wide receiver, a target for a quarterback. Still, he managed to rush for 697 total yards, but scored only two rushing touchdowns and three with pass receptions. Rauch could say,

"See. He's better at running with passes than out of the backfield." The Bills improved their record to four wins and ten losses.

The following year, the two rival leagues —AFL and NFL—finally merged and change was literally in the air. A refreshing new show began for the die-hard sports fan, when ABC-TV began Monday Night Football, with Howard Cosell, Don Meredith, and Keith Jackson sharing the microphone work. Now national television audiences would be able to see the premier NFL stars on Monday nights, from the comfort of their easy chairs. But if John Rauch sniffed change, he ignored it. The big development for the Buffalo Bills, as far as he was concerned, was the emergence of rookie quarterback Dennis Shaw, a fine passer. Again, O.J. Simpson was just another player in the mix. Halfway through the season, true to his determination that Simpson had to do almost everything but mop the floor, Rauch put O.J. in on a special teams situation that was similar to working on a suicide squad. O.J. did his best, but hurt his left knee and was forced to the sidelines. His rushing total for the year was only 488 yards and five touchdowns and the Bills cruised to a typical Rauch-like season of three wins, ten losses, and one tie.

The word was spreading around the league. Hey, remember O.J. Simpson, the flash from USC? He can't cut it in the big leagues. Even O.J. himself was beginning to doubt his ability, and having to live in the snow and ice of Buffalo, far from his beloved California sunshine, did not improve his disposition. He was stuck with a losing team that showed no sign of changing its style of play, and was carrying the ball a lousy fourteen times a game. He had seriously injured his knee doing a task to which he should never have been assigned. Was it time to quit, only two years into the contract?

The hardest position for Simpson to play was sitting on the bench, while Rauch filled the gloomy gray skies of creaky War Memorial Stadium in Buffalo with passes that never did the job. Instead of keying on the best running back in the league, the defenses simply concentrated on knocking down the thrown footballs of the pass-happy Bills. It was like shooting ducks in a barrel for a good team that could throw up zone coverages that were making long touchdown bombs obsolete.

But some players realized what was really

happening, and after a game with Denver, the Bronco's star running back Floyd Little comforted O.J., again an older person giving him sound advice. Little said things take time to adjust, and that his own first two seasons had been disasters. Then the Broncos got an offensive line and Little finally was able to run. He told O.J. not to quit. Hang in there. "Your day will come," Little said before heading to his locker room.

Finally, Rauch looked at what he had accomplished and realized that it wasn't much. Not much at all. Actually, he had squandered his most potent asset and had come close to driving O.J. Simpson out of football.

"The way Rauch used me just took all the fun out of the game. I wasn't happy because I wasn't carrying the ball. I felt my career was leaving me," Juice recalled. "You get down because you look around the league and see runners that aren't as good as you or no better, and they're doing so much better in the statistics. Some are carrying the ball fifty to one hundred times a season more than I was. I was used to carrying twenty, thirty times a game. After a lot of games in my first two years (at Buffalo) I wasn't even puffing. It's frustrating to feel so fresh after a game. . . . When you feel that fresh, you don't feel you've played a game or done anything for your team."

In one interview, Simpson said he only planned to stay in the league a couple of more years, then get out and work with troubled youths. Light suddenly appeared on the horizon, however, when Rauch did everyone a favor before the 1971 season began and quit.

Rauch had a parting shot however, saying that Simpson perhaps was playing in the real world. "With as fine a defense as USC had, they could afford to wait for O.J. to break the game open for them. But with Buffalo, we'd get down by fourteen points early in the game and we'd have to start playing catch-up. You can't play catch-up by giving the same guy the ball on every play and waiting for him to break one," he confidently declared. But he ignored the possibility that if he gave the ball to Simpson more in the early part of the game, perhaps the Bills wouldn't have fallen fourteen points behind in the first place.

Several years later in his career, Simpson did something very typical for him. He revised his criticism of Rauch, saying that some of the things that happened to him were his own fault, that he was a young man who made some mistakes.

But with Rauch gone, the management of the Buffalo Bills, never willing to sit on their hands when there was a chance to panic, decided to replace Rauch not with a big-name talented coach who could jump-start the team into aggressive play, but to bump scout and director of player personnel Harvey Johnson into the top coaching job for the time being. Everybody liked Johnson, the friendly front-office guy, and Simpson even referred to him as Uncle Harvey.

Johnson inherited disaster. He had to start five rookies in the first game, unheard of in the NFL, and his quarterback was the second-year Shaw, whose passing game abandoned him. The defense was almost nonexistent. What he had was a quality running back named O.J. Simpson who couldn't carry the load all by himself and was receiving precious little help, as the Bills spiraled downward through a season of one win and thirteen losses. O.J. rushed for 742 yards on 183 carries, scoring five touchdowns. He began to entertain thoughts of moving to another team where his special way of toting a football might be appreciated. Surely, somewhere in the league there was a team that needed a quality running back.

He would recall of those dark days that

the press was making excuses for him, but "the truth of the matter was that for three years, I hadn't done a thing. Nothing." He later admitted, "I was thinking about asking to be traded."

Then, as in theater plays in which the gods come down from heaven in the final act to make things right, Buffalo finally did something right.

5

DA BILLS

Lou Saban, who had led the Bills to an AFL championship in 1965, was convinced that something indeed might be possible with the sorry bunch of football players who wore the blue and white Buffalo uniforms. Saban had moved frequently as a coach, and since leaving the Bills had spent a year at the University of Maryland and then five with the Denver Broncos, where he helped develop Floyd Little's skills. So he came back to Buffalo like a man on a mission and laid his healing touch on O.J. Simpson. The clouds began to part and sunshine came again to Buffalo. "Lou was my first real coach in the pros," Simpson told *Newsweek*. "He turned us around and he saved my career."

Saban knew that Simpson was an exceptional talent, the sort that coaches get maybe once in a lifetime. And he quickly deciphered the secret that John McKay had unlocked at the University of Southern California. The more O.J. carried the ball, the stronger he got, the better he ran, the more productive a workhorse he became. A sportswriter recalled how Saban rewrote the script. "They had three plays. O.J. to the right, O.J. to the left, and O.J. up the middle. And it worked. Other teams knew what was coming but were helpless to stop it."

Even Saban couldn't patch all of the holes overnight and the Bills went into the 1972 season with a patchwork defense, a sudden nationwide hunt for bodies to replace wounded linemen, and one superstar. That did not deter the new head coach. He believed in the running game as fervently as Rauch had touted the forward pass, and he let O.J. carry the ball 291 times that season. Juice responded by gaining 1,251 yards—including one 94-yard gallop against Pittsburgh—to lead the league in rushing, scoring six touchdowns and helping the Bills improve to a record of four wins, nine losses, and one tie. That included three wins out of their final five games, because as O.J. got better, he carried the whole team along with him. "Coach Saban came to us with a winning attitude. He has changed the attitude of a lot of people," enthused O.J.

Simpson would get absolutely dreamy talking about running with a football tucked neatly in the crook of his arm. "You come through the line and it's a different world. One second you're hearing and seeing people and all of a sudden you're in the secondary, moving and juking. When you're facing a linebacker you just wiggle your body, watch him go off in one direction and you take off in the other."

He said his moves were instinctive, a feel for the ground and the situation that could not be planned in advance. "Somebody told me that he once asked [tennis great] Pancho Gonzalez what foot he hit his backhand off—and Pancho had to think about it before he answered. It's that way with a back. I can't always tell you what I did to get into the end zone." Whatever it was did not really matter. What did was the grace with which Juice ran, that supersonic glide that was poetry in football cleats. On film, it does not seem as if he is covering much ground until you notice how hard and fast the legs of the people chasing him are pumping, trying to catch up.

He ignored the possibility of being nailed

by some huge linebacker because he felt his job was to fake those people out of their cleats and leave them grasping at thin air, unable to get a clean hit. He laughingly called it his "okey-doke" move, bouncing around and looking for daylight rather than giving a linebacker a chance to rip off his head. "My game is to juke the tough guys," he said with a laugh.

He could joke about the jukes, but there was some steel in the backbone of O.J. Simpson. He was not afraid of any line-backer, any big defensive end, any corner-back, anybody. Simpson toned it down verbally, saying simply that all good ball-players had to be aggressive, and to be the best you had to be even more aggressive. Translated, that meant you had to be able to take a knock, and give one, and, perhaps, enjoy the tooth-rattling experience. O.J. Simpson walked onto a football field believing in the deepest recesses of his soul that he could whip any man on the pasture that day.

Mean Joe Greene, the stalwart Pittsburgh Steeler, finally had enough of Juice in one game several seasons later, when things had begun to click for the Juice. Mean Joe came up to the line of scrimmage and put one of his huge feet on the ball before the Bills' center could hike it to begin a play. "You can't have it. I'm not gonna let you play with it anymore," Greene barked. "That cat [Simpson] has done enough to us."

Mercury Morris, the fluid running back of the Miami Dolphins, discussed how having someone like Simpson made other running backs play harder. "It's much more satisfying when I do it against O.J.'s team," he said. "Back when I was in college, O.J. beat me out two years in a row for the collegiate rushing title. Simpson always seems to beat me out. When we play Buffalo, we always play the team, but for my own personal vendetta, I go against O.J."

Despite the Bills' new look, something had to be done to help O.J. and everyone in the league knew it. Simpson was beginning to fly, but he needed help in the trenches. The Bills had to get an offensive line that would give O.J. a fair chance at making decent yardage. Having a collection of the walking wounded for a line just wouldn't do. "I don't think he's even scratched the surface of his talent yet," observed Saban.

So on draft day in the Hotel Americana in New York, something extraordinary happened. Spectators gathered on a plaza to watch the men work their telephones, study their BLESTO sheets, and make their deals.

The improved Bills did not get to choose until the seventh spot in the first round.

Almost as if they were sitting in the Bills' stadium, watching Simpson run, the fans began to stamp and cheer and chant. "Get O.J. some blockers," they yelled. The fans had spoken. They didn't want a passer, nor a fleet wide receiver, nor another high-stepping running back, nor a kicker, nor anything or anyone else other than some bulls. "Get him a line!" they demanded of the draft overseers.

"Paul Seymour, tackle, Michigan," came the call when Buffalo made its pick. Those gathered on the terrace sent up a cheer that must have sounded like music to the ears of Saban and Simpson. What made it particularly interesting was that the people were not just Bills fans. They were football fans from all over, all of them fans of O.J. Simpson.

Saban pursued his rebuilding process as if it were a religious mission, bringing in such names as Reggie McKenzie, a second-year man out of Michigan; Seymour, chosen for his blocking ability and not his capabilities as a pass-catching tight end; returning lineman Donnie Green; Mike Montler from New England; Dave Foley in a trade with the New York Jets, and the outstanding right guard Joe DeLamielleure from Michigan State. They would quickly become known as The Electric Company because they were the ones who would turn on the Juice.

O.J.'s attitude improved so much that he began training months early for the coming 1973 season, an extraordinary campaign that would leave marvels all over the field. Donnie Green would later recall for *Time*, "Blocking for the Juice—Hey, man, there's no telling where he'll be. He moves so catty, moving to the left and then back to the right. I never know where the Juice is, but when I hear the roar of the crowd, I know he's gone!"

There was talk before the season began that O.J. now had the studs he needed working in front of him and that he could possibly break Jim Brown's single-year rushing mark of 1,863 yards. Perhaps most fans might have brushed it off as publicity hype by a dreadful team that was bursting to sell tickets after winning only a handful of games in the past four seasons. But Juice knew. He knew. And so did The Electric Company. And so did dandy rookie quarterback Joe Ferguson, a couple of glue-fingered new receivers and a beefed-up defense.

It did not take long for people to stand up and take notice of what was happening up in the frozen wastes of Buffalo, as O.J. Simpson went into his fifth season of professional football. In the first game, the Bills simply went out and throttled the New England Patriots, 31–13, with O.J. carrying the ball 29 times for a league single-game rushing record of 250 yards and scoring twice, once on an 80-yard jaunt.

Simpson was more than aware of the impossible goal he was chasing. Somewhere, a distant bell was ringing, intoning the challenge of the cocky street kid talking trash to football legend Jim Brown. *"You ain't so tough. I'm gonna to break all your records, suckah!"* Over the years of football, the kid had grown up and become friends with Brown, who had left football to become an actor in Hollywood. Brown held the record and Simpson wanted it.

Reporters constantly asked about the race and O.J. pointed toward the tall and talented front line that led the way, particularly the giant Reggie McKenzie. A familiar sight, one that brought Buffalo fans to their feet and drove enemy coaches to despair, was seeing the powerful McKenzie lumbering out in front of Simpson's famous number 32, splitting the hole between tackle and end. A sure ground gainer every single time. "The guys told me before the season that they'd get me 2,000 yards, and the way they're blowing tacklers out of my way, maybe we can do it."

As the historic season wore on, Simpson thrived like an orchid in a hothouse. Pictures show him walking back to a huddle, face turned up to the falling snow, his exhaled breath a vaporous balloon above a mouth sucking in air, but a man content, happy with his mission. They played fourteen games that year and only three times did O.J. not rush at least 100 yards, missing once by a single yard. And the crowd counted the results as closely as baseball fans of that summer had followed Henry Aaron's assault on Babe Ruth's home run record. They loved him. They needed him. The Game itself needed him, for it had spiraled into a conservative operation of field goals and tough defenses and coaches who played not to lose instead of to win. O.J. went against all that, a one-man wrecking crew who blazed new trails of excitement every Sunday afternoon of the season.

The last game of the year was at Shea Stadium, against the Joe Namath–led Jets, and the snow and mud presented serious obstacles to runners. O.J. and his pals knew what was on the line. He needed 61 yards to break the record. By the time it was over, the Bills had won 34–14, to finish 9–5 for the season, and O.J. had rushed into the Jets defense 34 times, dismantling a system designed to contain him, and racked up an even 200 yards. It smashed Brown's record and gave him 2,003 yards for the season, more than any player had ever amassed in the entire history of the league. For the year, O.J. averaged six yards per carry and led the league in rushing touchdowns with a dozen. Brown did not call to congratulate him, but O.J. said Brown had never called before then, so what was new?

Afterward, in the locker room, as reporters and cameramen jostled for position, O.J. showed his natural kindness in a dramatic way. He hauled the other ten members of the offensive team to his side and introduced them one by one to the frenzied media. "I want to introduce the cats who did the job all year," he said with a smile. "I hope to stay in the league until all these guys get old so no young back can get behind them and break the record."

Life seemed to be changing, and he even said he enjoyed Buffalo, although he continued to live in Los Angeles with his wife, their daughter, and a new son, Jason. His image was maturing, too, and he worked to help kids without seeking anything in return and regularly wrote checks for recreation centers, playgrounds, and youth programs.

Home may have been where his heart was, but Simpson's body was usually elsewhere. After his record-breaking season, he headed to Hawaii to cover the Hula Bowl for ABC-TV, dabbled in some acting, played in the Pro Bowl, and had offers to "more banquets than I know what to do with." And when he was home, away from the adulation and the spotlight, something very strange and out of character for this icon-in-the-making began to take place. His wife, Marguerite, began confiding to her closest friends that O.J., the man she had loved since high school, was mistreating her.

Such dirty laundry, whatever it was, was well hidden in the mid-seventies. Family matters and troubles stayed within the home, and to the outside world, O.J. was still presented as a man who had everything on track, a man who could do no wrong. He even went out of the way to prove that he was a good guy, that he had something to give back to the people who adored him, even in personal ways that were never meant for public consumption.

There was one instance where an exhausted Simpson returned to the field after a game to play catch with a child suffering from terminal cancer. No press was present. Another time, O.J. was parched after a game played in sweltering conditions and reporters surrounded him for almost an hour, until he had politely answered every question, joked with them in the mode of the jock fraternity, and sent them away happy to write more glowing stories. Someone handed him a cold drink at the same time he was told a little boy had waited outside the circle of reporters with a drink to give him and was about to go away disappointed. O.J. tossed his cold drink in the garbage, found the little boy and accepted the now-warm beverage, thanked him and drank it all on the spot. No press was present.

He seemed to know instinctively that there was going to be more to O.J. Simpson than football and that by making friends now, he could make money and a new life later. So instead of a morose and surly athlete, reporters always found an upbeat and happy Juice, a decent man who was cooperative, even when the media sharks were circling, never losing his temper. Reporters always prefer to talk to people who are friendly than people who bitch and moan at them. Such treatment of the Fourth Estate members costs nothing but time and patience and, as O.J. learned, publicity can be a very good thing indeed, as the media people several times voted him the most cooperative player in the National Football League. His flashing smile and handsome face began to pop up, not only in nightclubs with gold-chained friends or a seemingly endless stream of beautiful women who threw themselves in his path, but in the company of sober business executives in Brooks Brothers suits, men who would become his mentors in the life after football.

Actually, the true discovery of reality had come to him when things were looking as grim as they had ever gotten, back in the days when the Buffalo Bills could not buy a win with anything less than a threatened nuclear attack on the opposing team's stadium. Simpson had recalled that his mother always told him to turn things over to the Lord when the going really got tough, and he ended up visiting a chapel, listening to a talk by a visiting speaker.

As Newhouse described it in *Heisman: After the Glory*, Simpson experienced a professional epiphany.

"He was talking about businessmen, the kind who come to work before others and stay later. But even though they're putting in all that time, they have no idea where they're going. No goals. They're just spinning their wheels," Simpson recalled. "It hit me like a ton of bricks. I said to myself, 'This guy is talking about me!' All my life, I wanted fame and money, but I never stopped to think, 'What do I want now?' I've always been a positive guy, but it was that chapel meeting that put a focus on it. From that day, I began thinking what I wanted to be in football, and what I wanted to be when I left football, and really defining both."

Football could not last forever, not even for the most brilliant players, and he did not want to be just another over-the-hill jock with sore knees and a pocketful of memories when he hung up the football shoes.

In 1974, he was hobbled by an injury that held him to a mere 1,125 yards, a figure that most running backs in professional football never achieve, and the Bills finished 9–6 again. But that year the Bills went to the playoffs for the only time during Simpson's entire career, as a wild-card selection, and they were knocked off by the Pittsburgh Steelers, with the Steel Curtain defense actually holding the limping Simpson in check enough to limit the Buffalo running game to a mere 100 yards. Still, O.J. scored a touchdown, catching a short pass from Joe Ferguson. The new rival World Football League had started that year, attracting many established and new stars, but O.J. stayed put with the team that he had once regretted joining.

A good sign that nothing lasts forever and that fame was even fleeter than Juice on a good day came to him at the end of 1974. Buffalo sportswriters had to choose the city's Athlete of the Year, and they gave the award to tennis phenom Jimmy Arias, who was eleven years old.

It didn't matter as much by then because Juice was becoming more than a mere athlete. He was a hero, a self-appointed goodwill ambassador for an entire sport, and was buried beneath the most publicity given a football player since Broadway Joe Namath came on the scene in 1969.

The Juice came back strong, working with the maturing Electric Company, and led the league in rushing for the next two seasons. He had 1,817 yards in 1975, the year he also led the NFL with a rushing average of 5.5 yards per carry and rushing touchdowns, with 16, and another seven catching passes. He extolled revenge on the Steelers in the second game of the season, leading the Bills to a win behind his 227 rushing yards and an 88-yard run for a touchdown. The Bills finished with eight wins and six losses because of injuries to the defense that allowed opponents to rack up points as fast as Simpson.

Then Buffalo began to tinker with the strong pattern that seemed to be growing and that old nemesis, the forward pass, loomed large again. In 1976, a number of Bills regulars were given tickets out of town, and Simpson fell into a pit of gloom from which he managed to climb out on football Sundays to turn in another 1,503 yards rushing, leading the league once again and even posting his own single-game best mark of 273 yards against Detroit. Lou Saban was as disgusted as O.J., and five games into the season, he resigned as head coach, to be replaced by Jim Ringo.

O.J., however, was directly responsible for some of the 1976 slide in success. With the WFL still throwing money around, he wanted his share and the Bills became entangled in a huge contract dispute that included his demands to be traded. The Bills finally signed him to a three-year contract for $2.5 million, but the team had suffered extraordinary damage in morale. The Bills lost their last ten games of the season.

They started the 1977 season much the same way, out of tempo and out of time, losing their first four games. But even that disastrous start was but a mild tremor in comparison with the earthquake that rocked the team in the seventh game of the season, the day before Halloween. As the Seattle Seahawks humiliated the Bills, 56–17, O.J. Simpson sustained a major knee injury. The franchise player was down and out for the rest of the year and facing surgery to repair torn cartilage. It was déjà vu for Simpson. His team was back at the level where he began, finishing the year with three wins and eleven losses.

He was thirty years old, his football days were obviously numbered, his marriage was splitting at the seams, and he was struggling with personal questions about himself. He told *People* magazine at the time how he was "lonely and bored" when he wasn't around his family, and how he easily slipped into depression. "I often wondered why so many rich people commit suicide. Money sure isn't a cure-all," he said.

Marguerite, a shy and introverted woman, had finally reached her limit. She was quoted as saying, "We practically lost our private life. I have been shoved out of the way, pushed and stepped on by more than one beautiful woman. I admit I'm jealous." O.J., the dashing extrovert, did not contradict her. He said only that he was "more selective" these days in which groupies he picked for company. "My wife knows I'm under control."

But she was getting very, very tired of his antics and felt it was time for the man whom the world thought was so great to ease out of the spotlight of public adulation, come home, settle down, and be a good husband and father to their three children. It was like asking a dog to climb a tree. It wasn't going to happen. A separation followed. O.J. was free to roam.

The savvy and experienced Chuck Knox took over as Bills' coach for 1978 and helped put together a major deal. Buffalo traded Simpson, his extraordinary skills obviously diminished, to the San Francisco 49ers for a package of five nice draft choices with which he would start his own rebuilding program. A new era was dawning and he tore up the old meal ticket.

For Simpson, it was like being thrown a lifeline at the end of a long swim. He was now on the field with the 'Niners, not in the end-zone stands. He was returning to his beloved West Coast, carrying the biggest salary in the NFL. Although he was past his prime, he would earn $733,358 for the year whether he played a down or not, and the contract would cough up another $806,668 the following year. "Home at last," he called to reporters who came for a news conference. "Thank God Almighty, I'm home at last."

The 49ers considered the contract a bargain, because they needed someone who could put fans in the seats, and O.J. was not only a hometown boy, but a superstar. But he was only a ghost of his former playing self and knee and shoulder problems plagued him through a season in which he recorded 593 yards rushing, enough to make an average running back proud, but a set of numbers that only brought dismay to Simpson.

Just when he thought things could not get any worse, during training camp in 1979 as he prepared for what would be his eleventh and last season, he received news of a domestic tragedy. His 23-month-old daughter, Aaren, had fallen into the swimming pool at Marguerite's home and died about a week later. It was reported by *Time* that he ran through the hospital corridors yelling, "She murdered my child! She murdered my child!" In fact, it was a tragic accident.

The birth of a daughter had marked the start of his meteoric professional career when he won the Heisman, and the death of a daughter came at the end of it.

There were more physical problems that season and O.J. completed only 460 yards rushing and a mere three touchdowns. In his final game, against Tampa Bay, the 49ers honored the man who was now a legend. Among the people that Simpson publicly thanked that day was the coach of the opposing team, John McKay, his old coach from USC.

It is true that O.J. Simpson was hobbled when he finally left the football field and fame behind him. But no one had ever walked in such shoes before. For five consecutive seasons, he rushed for more than 1,000 yards and was, when he retired, the only player *ever* to gain more than 2,000.

For his career, he had rushed 2,404 times in 11 NFL seasons for 11,236 yards and an average of 4.1 yards per carry. He scored 61 touchdowns rushing, 14 catching passes and returned one kickoff all the way. His 203 passes added another 2,142 yards to his real estate total, and the 333 kickoffs tacked on still another 990 yards. As the calendar was turning, *Pro Football Monthly* named him the Player of the Decade. And in his first year of eligibility, 1985, he would be named to the Professional Football Hall of Fame in Canton, Ohio.

6

CAMERAS

There would be no more days of O.J. Simpson striding out onto a football field, dressed in his uniform, pads, and cleats, ready to put a hurting on another team, while the fans, tens of thousands of them, would rock the stadium yelling his name. *Juice! Juice! Juice!* For most professional athletes, such a time is the end of the line, and among the ranks of the gifted few who make it to the pro leagues, a sense of dispirited failure wafts after them like a bad smell, no matter what the accomplishments of their youth. Such men were paid well and provided entertainment for America in return for those hefty paychecks, and they enjoyed the camaraderie of the sweaty locker rooms. Then, when the skills eroded and a new crop of kids ambled onto the scene, hungry for their jobs, it was suddenly good-bye and thanks for playing.

But O.J. wasn't like most athletes. He had known for years that he would thrive long after his illustrious NFL career was over, because he had prepared to do so.

With his personality, intelligence, bright smile, physique, engaging wit and easy way of bantering, Simpson invited the cameras closer. Instead of scrambling around on the gridiron, he was now standing there holding a microphone as a television commentator, or pursuing his other blossoming career in Hollywood as an actor, or making commercials for corporate America. Millions of football fans had known him for his touchdowns and dramatic runs. Now millions more people who had never followed his athletic career became captivated by the magnetic charm of O.J. Simpson, who wore his television personality as easily as he wore the expensive, tailored clothing that molded to his sculpted body. No matter what he was selling, the audience liked who was selling it. *Yeah! It's O.J.* He became a household name.

Hollywood had already gone through the awful black exploitation films of the early seventies, when white screenwriters tried and failed to create African-American super-heroes. *Shaft* had made a breakthrough fortune, and soon such films were rolling off the production block at a dime-a-dozen rate, featuring almost any black athlete who wanted to take a shot at the movie biz, as long as they were willing to talk jive, wear bushy Afro haircuts, and portray violence. The music was usually good, but the characters were too artificial, too far removed from the gritty reality of everyday black life in America to be truly successful, and the genre soon faded into movie trivia.

That did not mean that there were not black actors and actresses with immense talent, and such performers as Ossie Davis, Ruby Dee, Richard Rountree, Morgan Freeman, Lou Gossett, Jr., and Denzel Washington would continually prove over the coming years. However, at the precise time Simpson was developing his side jobs while playing football, Hollywood considered black actors to be in the mold of the glowering, towering Jim Brown. The former football great had latched his star onto films at the end of his own illustrious career and, while he made several motion pictures, he kept the image of a tough, mean black man. Even if he tried to be friendly to a white actor on the screen, it seemed as if he were growling.

He was a proud black man, and an imposing figure who became almost a symbol of the racial divisions that were affecting the country. It crystallized in a movie in which the brawny Brown played a love scene with Raquel Welch, buxom, beautiful, and white, who was topless. When the scene sparked controversy later, she insisted later that a towel actually separated the otherwise naked tops of their bodies. White America watched and cringed. Not only was the issue explosive, but the movie was lousy.

Then through the same football door strolled O.J. Studio executives looked him over. Now, *here* was a black man that might be able to sell tickets and popcorn. He was not nearly so the threatening, he had automatic magnetism, he was articulate, he was already among the few people in America known by their first names—in his case, his initials—and he truly wanted to be a good actor. Brown represented all of that Black Power stuff. O.J. represented sweetness and light.

O.J., like he was coming out of the backfield, got off to a roaring start in the cinematic, never-never land of Hollywood, and landed a role in a hospital drama called

Medical Center before he ever played a game for the Bills. His first feature film role came in 1974, when he landed a part in *The Towering Inferno* and his name went up in lights beside that of film greats Steve McQueen and Paul Newman. When Alex Haley's megahit television series *Roots* was cast in 1977, O.J. was a natural, along with a galaxy of established stars who helped American viewers cross the color line in theater arts. As if to make certain that America was comfortable with this new black presence, in 1974 Simpson filmed an otherwise trite "passions flare and violence erupts in the Deep South" cliché motion picture called *The Klansman*, and got to study the moves of Richard Burton, Lee Marvin, and Lola Falana. It worked. Simpson was nearing his peak as a football player at the time, but already Hollywood considered him to be what the studios call "bankable." His new career was assured.

Killer Force followed in 1975, and two years later, he made two movies, *A Killing Affair* and *The Cassandra Crossing*. Perhaps his most memorable movie of those years was *Capricorn One*, made in 1978. It was a ridiculous story line, with the U.S. government pulling a hoax about the first spaceflight to Mars, but the cast turned it into a romp that obtained a cult following. O.J. Simpson was now seeing his name in big letters on motion picture screens along with *Capricorn* co-stars Eliott Gould, Brenda Vaccaro, Sam Waterson, Hal Holbrook, and Telly Savalas.

Simpson realized, however, that he was being type-cast, and accepted that role. As he told the *Washington Post*, "Obviously, I'm not a Dustin Hoffman. I have to play an athletic type, just as Woody Allen has to play a wimpy type. No matter how many acting lessons I took, the public just wouldn't buy me as Othello."

The pay was outstanding, particularly when combined with the monstrous bucks he was pulling down playing football, but, more important, Hollywood kept calling his agent. It didn't matter if O.J. still appeared stiff in many of the situations, or that he sometimes lapsed into a guttural tone that could barely be understood. He was taking voice and acting lessons and the producers wanted him for more featured screen and television movie roles. Simpson was money in the bank for a project. And every time he appeared on the screen for the first scene in any move, the audience saw their handsome, friendly pal doing well. *O.K., O.J.!*

The last year of the decade, with football

all but behind him, was a big one for Simpson on the sound stage. He made three motion pictures that year—*Firepower, Goldie and the Boxer,* and *Goldie and the Boxer Go to Hollywood.* Obviously, scripts were a problem, as producers and writers tried to find a niche for this new talent.

In the 1980s, he expanded into other commitments and businesses, but still made time in 1980 for *The Golden Moment: An Olympic Love Story,* and part of an HBO sitcom about football called *First and Ten.* In 1984, he was in a piece of fluff called *Hambone & Hillie.* In 1987, he played in a couple of dogs entitled *Student Exchange* and *Cocaine and Blue Eyes.* After making movies for sixteen years, he still had not really able to achieve the kind of leading man status that the surly Jim Brown had briefly attained and the filmmaking community, always ready to devour one of their own, wondered if the bright promise of O.J. Simpson was a false promise. Everyone knew him and everyone liked him, but, damn, you gotta watch the box office receipts and Juice seemed to be losing his touch as a ticket attraction.

Just like so many football coaches, the filmmakers had simply miscast O.J. Simpson, trying to make him fit their version of what he should be. Like the coaches, they stumbled onto success. Simpson was a guy who liked people, liked to make them laugh, liked to laugh with them, right? Why not try him in a comedy? In 1988, director David Zucker and his writing partners came up with the daft idea of doing a movie spinoff of an old television series that spoofed the serious and glamorous stories of police officers and created *The Naked Gun—From the Files of Police Squad!*

O.J. Simpson was cast as Detective Nordberg, a goofy sidekick of lamebrain Lieutenant Frank Drebin, played deadpan by snow-haired Leslie Nielsen. Simpson is shot, doused with wet paint, has a window slam shut on his fingers and a bear trap clamp onto his leg. The audience roared with laughter as he took the pratfalls with a benign and innocent look on his face. The producers sat back and watched the money roll in. O.J. had found his niche, once again by being just what he really was, a nice, warm, and funny guy. He came back for the 1991 sequel *Naked Gun 2½—The Smell of Fear*, and also in 1994 in the third part of this trilogy of PG-13 silliness, *Naked Gun 33⅓—The Final Insult.* With this move, O.J.

could stop worrying about having to be Hamlet and happily settle for being a ham.

Movies were not his only work before the cameras. Advertisers had long discovered that the athlete was so well-liked that he made a tremendous pitchman for their products. People liked O.J., so why wouldn't they like what O.J. had to peddle? With that rationale, and the demographic numbers that showed his success, the endorsement and advertising offers rolled in, accompanied by wheelbarrow loads of cash.

Naturally, there had to be one orange juice company, Tree Sweet, and as the years progressed, he pitched MCI telephone services, including a memorable commercial in which his mother is shown jumping over a sofa in her living room dash to answer a telephone call from her son. That was a spinoff some of the commercials that O.J. made for Hertz, the rental-car company.

They started him as a spokesperson in 1979 at the end of his football days and the commercials clicked immediately as Juice told audiences that the company was the Superstar of Rent-A-Car. Americans loved the advertisements of O.J. sprinting through airports, vaulting over chairs while astonished fellow passengers gaped at the star in their midst. In the 1990s, he was charging Hertz $200,000 per brief commercial and the company gladly shelled out the money. The dark fear of all advertisers is that television viewers will remember the gag or the spokesperson and forget the product. Not so in this case, and the numbers showed that an astounding 90 percent of Americans thought of Hertz when they thought of O.J., which was frequently. Simpson was closing in on the record of the Energizer Bunny, the most popular and recognized advertising celebrity in the world.

By now, one might think that enough was enough!

O.J. had conquered college football, had been named Player of the Decade in professional football, become an idol and role model for millions of underprivileged kids of all races, made a name for himself as a motion picture actor, and apparently had the ability to sell almost anything to anybody as a TV huckster. He had more money than some small countries, was one of the most recognized people in America if not the world, and wore all of his achievements with the quiet grace of The Original Mister Nice Guy.

Wrong. There was still one more thing

that O.J. Simpson was doing to earn a couple of bucks, and it perhaps won him more attention than all the rest. He became a television sportscaster.

He had been doing the sideline and color stuff for mid-level games as a tyro in the business with ABC-TV ever since he had left USC and won a long-term contract from sports broadcasting impresario Roone Arledge. Wide World of Sports and Bowl games, primarily, since the Buffalo Bills were always knocked out of post-season contention early and regularly enough for ABC to schedule him into the broadcasting lineup.

"Monday Night Football" had become an American staple, like toast and coffee. But after several years on the tube, a new character was added to the broadcast team in 1983. O.J. Simpson went prime time, working as a color analyst, the announcer who usually spends a game describing the obvious. For two years, he was part of the announcing team that brought football into millions of American homes every week throughout the season.

As always, he got better the longer he did the job. The voice lessons and acting classes paid off and his diction improved steadily, making his talent and knowledge even more valuable. It did not hurt that he was a black broadcaster of a sport that was dominated by black players. Starting in 1990, he was the co-host of *NFL Live* on NBC-TV with Bob Costas.

And he still seemed to have stumbled onto the planet by accident. Nobody who had achieved so much could possibly be such a good guy. But he was. "He's one of the nicest guys I've ever met. He'll give you the shirt off his back," said *NFL Live* analyst Will McDonough, who has known thousands of athletes and broadcasters in a long career as a sportswriter.

He was standing atop the pyramid, a place that 99.9 percent of the population could not reach, not even in their dreams. He was a multimillionaire. He had power. He played golf with Arnold Palmer and went to the wedding of Donald Trump and Marla Maples. Entertainment magazines loved him. Simpson had done about everything but invent a way to spin gold from straw, and had succeeded at everything he put his hand to, except that marriage with Marguerite.

The past was amazing and his future unlimited. Rarely in America had the rags-to-riches story been told in the public eye as it had been by a down-to-earth guy with the strange name of Orenthal James Simpson. And it seemed as if the entire country was still up in the stands, rooting for him, cheering his every success. The merry way in which he answered a telephone said it all. "Juice here. Go."

A factor that made his media success so interesting was that O.J. Simpson is a black man who was making it big in white America and the subject of race was hardly ever mentioned. Indeed, the demographic studies showed that race was not the first thing that came to people's minds when they saw him. "Hertz told me in all their surveys that I was colorless," he told an interviewer in 1992.

He was, however, a product of his time in an America that has never been color-blind. Growing up on Potrero Hill plainly showed him there was a gulf between where he lived in gritty conditions and where the wealthy whites lived up on Nob Hill, overlooking San Francisco Bay.

The difference was that he did not let the racial issue poison or polarize him, a rather astonishing feat in itself in the turbulent decade of the sixties. In 1965, the year O.J. graduated from high school, Dr. Martin Luther King, Jr., staged his famous march from Selma to Montgomery, Alabama, to protest discrimination against blacks in voting. In Los Angeles, blacks rioted for six days in Watts. Two years later, when he started at USC, riots by blacks flattened and burned areas of Cleveland, Detroit, Newark, Boston, New Haven, and other cities. Thurgood Marshall became the first black justice to sit on the U.S. Supreme Court. In 1968, the year that he became only the third black player ever to win the Heisman, Dr. King was assassinated in Tennessee.

O.J. Simpson would have had to be blind and unfeeling not to have such momentous events touch him. Black militancy was gripping the country even as the United States struggled with the faraway war in Vietnam and the challenges to established authority underway on the home front. And Simpson had to make some decisions.

On February 15, 1968, the New York Athletic Club, which had no black members, staged a track meet that was to be a preliminary event to the XIX Olympiad in Mexico City later that year. Already there had been a push for a black boycott of the Olympic Games, with only moderate success among the black athletes. To put teeth into the boycott threat, some black organizations wanted to use the New York meet as an example of their clout. The day of the races, the International Olympics Committee decided in France to allow South Africa to participate in the Olympics. The decision lit a fuse, and in New York, high schools, the military service academies, and the Soviet Union withdrew from the meet. Activist H. Rap Brown proposed that Madison Square Garden should be blown up in protest. O.J. was not prepared to carry any dynamite, but was adamant about not crossing the picket line. "I wouldn't run in that weekend [race] if my mother was holding the meet," Juice declared.

During the Olympics, the world watched on television as victorious black American runners Tommie Smith and John Carlos thrust their clenched fists high in protest, a visible signal that black athletes were firmly in the camp of militant change.

Just as the public was getting anxious about Black Power, along came O.J. to almost defuse the problems singlehandedly. While running with the football for the next decade, he also poured soothing balm on the racial conflicts wracking the country. In later years, the same sort of idolatry would be offered to athletes such as Magic Johnson, Michael Jordan, and Shaquille O'Neal, all smiling and genial athletes that would be easily adopted by white America. O.J. was the first of the breed, out there cracking open the world of lucrative commercial endorsements, peddling tennis shoes, guzzling soft drinks, and telling people they ought to rent from Hertz.

There was no doubt in the minds of the fans and the consumers that O.J. was black, but the public bonded with him as it had never done with a black athlete before. Not with Jackie Robinson, not Roy Campanella, not Jim Brown. O.J. built a pedestal for himself and then stood proudly up there, waving to *all* Americans, regardless of their race. Heck, they even liked his strange name.

In one particularly bizarre incident, recalled by *New York Times* columnist Robert Lipsyte, O.J. mused on how he seemed to have transcended the subject of race. "My biggest accomplishment is that people look at me like a man first, not a black man. I was at a wedding, my wife and a few friends were the only Negroes there, and I overheard a lady at the next table say, 'Look, there's O.J. Simpson and some niggers.' "

The reflective column also demonstrated that O.J. had indeed spent a great deal of time considering the paradox of his success and the color of his skin. "That sort of thing hurts me, even though it's what I strive for," Simpson said of the wedding party incident. "Maybe it's money, a class thing. The Negro is always identified with poverty. But then you think of Willie Mays as black, but not Bill Cosby. So it's more than just money. As black men we need something up there all the time for us, but what I'm doing is not for principles or black people. No, I'm dealing first for O.J. Simpson, his wife and his baby."

O.J. worked hard at creating and maintaining that image of a friendly, nonthreatening person, someone who could succeed in life and not become trapped by either racial or athletic stereotypes. In his book *O.J.: The Education of a Rich Rookie*, Simpson wrote, "I became very aware of my image. After taking so long to find out who I was, I didn't want anyone else to misunderstand me. I didn't want to be O.J. Simpson, running back. I wanted to be O.J. Simpson, a good guy. I'm happy to admit it; I really enjoy being liked. I loved it when kids stopped me for autographs. I loved it when people recognized me on the street. I loved it, I think because I could at last recognize myself." He was his own best cheerleader and constantly surrounded himself with, and cultivated, friends of all races.

He even developed the ability to actually joke about race, and make people laugh with him, not at him. One day in Oakland, California, he was making a television commercial and because he was so close to the neighborhood turf of his youth, Simpson lapsed into the jive jargon of the streets, according to *Newsweek*. He stopped the shoot, angry at the slip, then recorded the commercial perfectly on the second effort. Afterward, he brushed off the incident. "That's what happens when I spend too much time with my boys. I forget how to talk white."

Even if some people looked askance at O.J. and his dazzlingly white second wife, he was able to let it slide because he saw absolutely nothing unique in his relationship with Nicole, because to O.J. racism was somebody else's problem. Even with his success and bushels of money falling on him because white people thought he was about the greatest thing since sliced bread, O.J. never for a moment forgot his roots. He contributed money for recreational facilities on Potrero Hill and regularly would surprise old friends who had not escaped the pull of the ghetto with telephone calls, tickets to games, or gifts. The guy they had known as a backstreet hustler would invite them down to Los Angeles for a party, no excuses accepted, the tickets are waiting at the airport. His house and his parties were always open to his friends of the distant past.

O.J. Simpson has never shirked his race. He just never let it slow him down. In fact, he never let anything slow him down.

In the incredible drama that was to explode in his life in 1994, throughout the unprecedented media coverage, it was hardly ever mentioned that O.J. Simpson was black. What was emphasized was that he was a genuine American hero.

7

NICOLE

O.J. Simpson played many parts well, but the one important role that seemed to be totally beyond him was that of a good husband. He had failed with Marguerite, but giving things a second effort had been his lifelong trademark and he was not afraid to give marriage another try. The only questions were who and when.

In 1977, while he was still playing pro football, O.J. was in a Los Angeles restaurant called The Daisy and the waitress serving him was a breathtaking, willowy blond teenager with flawlessly tanned skin. Everything about her was gorgeous, from the flashing eyes to the knockout figure. The 30-year-old O.J. soon asked 18-year-old Nicole

Brown, who stood only a head shorter than him, for a date.

A new and thrilling world suddenly opened for the young Nicole. She was just out of high school in Dana Point, a beach community of Orange County south of Los Angeles where attractive blond girls like her usually paired off with equally blond surfer boys. Born in Frankfurt, Germany, and raised in California, she had been a vibrant and socially active girl, filled with thoughts of the future when she might become a fashion model. One fellow student recalled that there was an aura about the tall blond girl, who knew "she was going to go somewhere and be somebody." Such dreams are common to young girls before they leave school and home and meet the real, uncompromising world.

The highlight of her life until now had been her selection in 1976 as a princess in the high school homecoming court. After high school, she moved to the Los Angeles area of Westwood, near UCLA, and began to work as a waitress. Suddenly, a year later, after only being able to land a job as a waitress, she was being squired about to glittering nightclubs by a handsome black superstar athlete and movie star who dropped dollar bills on her like an avalanche of soft green leaves. The fact that he was still married, the dozen-year difference in their ages, and the even more startling difference in their skin color raised eyebrows among some of their friends, but O.J. and Nicole were head over heels in love and could have cared less what anyone else thought. Their attraction was immediate, their desire for one another seemingly unquenchable.

In an extraordinarily prescient comment, Simpson told *Heisman* author Dave Newhouse, "You say to yourself that it's a blink of the eye that you're here on earth. The blink of an eye. I mean, who cares? I've got one person in the world who I have to please, and that's me." Interestingly, he did not say that he had to please Nicole.

Almost immediately after meeting Simpson, Nicole's career as a waitress came to an end and the sunny, charming girl moved out of her small Westwood apartment and into her new boyfriend's huge mansion in the posh Los Angeles enclave of Brentwood. Behind walls and a gate, servants paid attention to her every whim, she was given cars and money and trips to exotic places, and was taken by O.J. to the parties of the elite in the entertainment, sports and media worlds. The spotlights shown constantly on them and the strikingly beautiful teen made a perfect princess, while his handsome darkness complimented the paleness of her German ancestry. They were treated like royalty wherever they went.

After the divorce between Marguerite and O.J. had become final in 1979, and having lived with him since 1978, Nicole married O.J. in a private ceremony beneath a tent on the lawn of his huge Brentwood home in February 1985, three months after the gorgeous woman signed a prenuptial agreement that stated if they ever broke up, she would not be able to claim his fortune of some $10 million at that time, nor several properties. The money issue was not the concern of some of his close advisers, who worried instead about his image, how other African-Americans would react to one of the nation's most well known black men marrying a young white girl. O.J. said that people should be left alone to fall in love with the person of their choice, whomever it is that can make them truly happy. If other people had problems with that, well, those dilemmas were not the problems of O.J. and Nicole.

There was no doubt that they were deeply in love. One photo from the early years of their marriage shows them in front-row seats at a sporting event, a Pepsi-Cola cup in her left hand. Her head is thrown back, blond hair cascading over the seat, and her right arm is outstretched to pull O.J.'s head down to her lips for a big public kiss. Passion, good and bad, was never absent in their relationship.

The year of 1985 was a big one for O.J., for not only did he remarry, but that year he was inducted in the Pro Football Hall of Fame, along with center Frank Gatski, quarterbacks Joe Namath and Roger Staubach and NFL Commissioner Pete Rozelle. His beautiful new wife was in the audience, dressed in a sky blue outfit with her blond hair swept back and gazing up with pride at the legend who was her husband, sharing his glory and triumph. O.J., as usual, was as gracious as a person could be. He was being given the highest honor in the profession and he said it was directly due to the other players who had helped him every step of the way. Then he singled out a special woman in his life with a stirring, emotional comment. But first, he had something nice to say about the rest of his family.

Looking down at Eunice Simpson, who had worked the hospital graveyard shift for so many years, put three meals on the table, and kept a public housing project home together, O.J. spoke with pride.

"I want to thank my family. I see my sister Shirley, Carmelita, my brother Truman. Because no matter what I was, if I was a window washer or a bus driver, they all would make me feel just as loved. My kids, no one could ask for better kids, more loving kids. They keep me on my toes, as any teenager kids would. I love them. My wife, Nicole, who came into my life at what is probably the most difficult time for an athlete, at the end of my career. And she turned those years into some of the best years I have had in my life, Babes.

"My dad Jimmy, well what do you say about your dad? There are people who are raised in broken homes. Even though my dad didn't live under the same roof as us during most of my youth, he was always there, Dad. He was always there, I always had a problem. I love you for it . . .

"I don't know what you say about the most important person in your life, I'm just glad she is here today. My mother. I mean, you just don't know what it is to be 8 years old and have all your friends think that you have the best mother in the neighborhood. I remember when I was about 9 years old. My mother worked all her life and she took the family on vacation to visit her sister in Las Vegas and she had two weeks off.

"She worked the graveyard shift in San Francisco General Hospital for 30-something years. And while we were down there about five days into the vacation, I had to play in my first Little League baseball game. And I was moping around and she noticed how sad I was. And, I don't know, she drove me 700 miles in the middle of vacation, she took me 700 miles back to San Francisco so I wouldn't miss my first Little League game. I know I wouldn't be here now if it wasn't for my mother's prayers."

Whatever Nicole wanted, she could have, and she indulged herself in good times. There was travel to exciting places, a $1.9-million beachfront home in tony Laguna Beach, ski vacations to the mountains of Vail, Colorado, and a yearly visit to Hawaii. The best hotels, the best seats in the best restaurants, expensive automobiles, and fawning service provided by the full staff of servants at the opulent mansion in Brentwood.

Also living in the Simpson estate was O.J.'s son, Jason, with daughter Arnelle spending part of her time there, too. Even Marguerite, the first wife, lived nearby. The house was always full of friends, and Nicole would stay busy in the kitchen fixing food for the visitors. O.J. said she enjoyed doing so.

Both O.J. and Nicole wanted to start a family of their own immediately, with Juice saying that he wasn't around much when his first children were growing up, but all of that was going to change, he could guarantee it. Shortly after their wedding, their first child, Sydney Brooke, arrived. Three years later came a son, Justin.

There is a price, however, for everything and the amount to be paid is not always measured in dollars.

For Nicole, the price was being a trophy wife, someone to be displayed with pride. O.J. was jealous and so possessive that he forced her to drop out of junior college so she could constantly be at his side. Her only career was to be Mrs. O.J. Simpson. But that did not seem to be a two-way street with him, and O.J.'s former high school chum Joe Bell said women constantly threw themselves at him. As Marguerite had before her, Nicole felt jealous and helpless. "I know from talking to Nicole that it was a problem," said Bell.

Something even more serious was wrong with the relationship, however, and their marriage became tempestuous. Responses to the exclusive Simpson residence in Brentwood began to show up on police blotters and the noise of their arguments could be heard by neighbors. "It's an ongoing problem," said one cop of the visits to the mansion, but it was not new behavior for the Simpsons. One of Nicole's old neighbors in Westwood remembered hearing the apparently hot-tempered couple shouting at each other even when they were courting. Friends said they noticed marks on Nicole but were reluctant to say anything.

The superstar's abuse of his wife exploded into public view in the pre-dawn hours of New Year's Day, 1989. Police once again received a 911 call to the Simpson household from Nicole and upon arriving, the officers were astonished to find a bruised and bleeding Nicole, clad only in sweat pants and a bra, hiding in the bushes. She ran to the gate to let them inside, clung to the officers as if they were saving her from drowning, and wept, "He's going to kill me, he's going to kill me."

A shouting O.J. Simpson appeared at the front door in his bathrobe, demanding to know why the cops were making such a big deal of this particular incident, which, after all, was just a "family matter." Other cops had been to the house many other times and nothing had ever been done. "I don't want this woman sleeping in my bed anymore. I've got two women and I don't want that woman in my bed anymore!" he shouted. Then O.J. jumped into his Bentley and fled the scene. The cops asked if O.J. had a gun, Nicole told them that "He's got lots of guns." They went after him.

Newspapers and television stations had a brief field day with the story, but it quickly faded. Still, it was the first really bad publicity that O.J. had ever received, and he was shocked at how the worshipful media he had known in the sports and entertainment realms did not exist among hard-nosed news reporters. Didn't they know he was one of them, a TV personality himself? The news types shrugged. To them, he was just someone else who got nabbed for beating up his wife, although *who* he was made it even more interesting. It was a situation that would be repeated many times within a few years.

In court, Nicole refused once again to press charges against O.J. Deputy City Attorney Robert Pingle cared even less about how Simpson felt. Pingle had seen the terrified Nicole the night of the incident and was shocked by the black eye, the bruise on her forehead, the neck scratches, and the swollen cheek of the woman. He wanted O.J. to learn a hard lesson, and suggested the court hand down a sentence of 30 days in jail because Simpson had shown absolutely no remorse over severely beating his wife. Pingle filed charges of spousal battery.

O.J. entered a plea of no contest, essentially not pleading either guilty nor innocent. On May 24, 1989, an apparently star-struck municipal judge in West Los Angeles gave Simpson a sentence of two years' probation and ordered him to pay a $200 fine, donate $500 to a battered women's shelter, perform some 120 hours of community service, and get some psychiatric counseling.

The fine and donation did not exactly wipe out O.J.'s bank account, and he virtually ignored the court order to do community service. Pingle hauled him back in for parole violation and an arrogant Simpson told the judge, "I've done more community service than anyone in this courthouse." Nevertheless, he had to complete the assigned sentence, in which he was allowed to partake of psychiatric counseling at his convenience, by telephone. His lawyer was Howard Weitzman, who was a close friend and would figure significantly in future proceedings. The judge in the case lived in Brentwood, not far from the Simpson estate. The lenient sentence by the court left a trail of seething anger among prosecutors who were trying to get the judges to pay attention to the awful problem of spousal abuse.

In later years, O.J. objected to the cloud of notoriety that had been brought by the incident. In an interview on ESPN, he said it "was not a big fight," just one that got "a little loud" at 3 A.M. He told the interviewer that he and Nicole had patched things up so quickly that within hours, after the Rose Bowl game on New Year's Day, they threw a party and everyone had a great time. With a deprecating nod, he said the whole thing was embarrassing.

Nicole sought professional advice after the incident and eventually wound up seeing Susan Forward, therapist author of a best-selling book about battered wives, *Men Who Hate Women and the Women Who Love Them*. Forward listened in shock as Nicole Simpson told her how an obsessed O.J. terrorized her, pulling her hair, slapping and kicking and beating her, threatening to kill her.

Their relationship deteriorated from that point and all efforts to start anew failed as they whirled downward in a love-hate spiral, the feuds and reconciliations becoming part of an ongoing tapestry. "He beat her all through the marriage and after they were separated, he would stalk her," Forward recalled later. "He would say things to her like, 'If I can't have you then no one can.' "

Julianne Hendricks, a friend of the Brown family, told the television show *Inside Edition* of a 1990 incident that proved O.J. had not learned whatever lesson Pingle had hoped to teach him about beating women. He was drunk when she was introduced, and "not the charismatic person I had seen on television," and as the evening wore on, he drank even more, as did Nicole. When it came time to go home, it was clear that O.J. was too inebriated to drive his Rolls-Royce and Nicole agreed to let someone else take the keys. Hendricks said that when everyone was in the car, O.J. became furious with Nicole, who was sitting beside him in the front seat, and began to curse and slap her. Then, with the car moving, he opened the door of the car and pushed her out. The following morning, Hendricks was told by others not to take the incident seriously, for that sort of thing happened all the time with the Simpsons.

* * *

Three years later, on March 23, 1992, *Jet* magazine carried a photograph of the couple and a brief story that said: "After a tumultuous seven-year marriage that included charges of wife-beating, football Hall of Fame inductee and television sportscaster O.J. Simpson was recently hit with divorce papers by his white wife, Nicole."

Her lawyers pointed out, without success, that because of her relationship with O.J., who demanded all of her attention and time, she had developed no skills with which to cope with the real world. The waitress job was long gone, as was an attempt at being a sales clerk on Rodeo Drive, when she sold absolutely nothing. "These two jobs are the sum total of her employment experience," her lawyers argued, as they sought a court decree that would allow her to maintain the "exceptionally affluent" lifestyle that she had enjoyed for the past seven years of their married life. She asked the divorce court for $40,000 a month and listed regular expenses, such as a $3,200 monthly budget for designer clothes and $2,500 for pet care, hair care, toys, and gifts.

But the prenuptial agreement they had signed so long ago went into legal effect and shot down most of her attempts. She was awarded a lump-sum settlement of

$435,750, a luxury condominium at 875 South Bundy Drive, not far from Simpson's home, and $10,000 a month in child support. The court gave her custody of her two children.

Finally, the marriage of seven years came to an end, but certainly not their relationship. He was 44 years old and still handsome, and Nicole was 35 and still beautiful.

8

ABUSE

Seldom has such a deep, dark secret as wife abuse suddenly been drenched by so much publicity. For generations, an uncommon number of married women have been regularly, and at times terribly, beaten by their husbands, and nothing was said. It has only been in recent years that the issue of spousal abuse has changed from being considered just a "family matter" and elevated to what it actually is, a terrible slice of violent crime that is repeated and repeated and repeated within the same households until some tragic consequence ends it.

The two questions that arose immediately in the minds of a shocked public that had begun to follow every nuance of the Simpson case were: Did O.J. really beat Nicole?

And if he did, why didn't she leave him much earlier?

Although some still question it, the police documents speak for themselves. Certainly, Nicole was so battered and bruised after the fight of New Year's Day, 1989, that O.J. had been arrested, tried, and sentenced for the crime. Certainly, police had been running out to settle problems at the mansion during the marriage, and to her town house after the divorce.

Still, it may not be as simple an equation as it seems. O.J. had repeatedly told friends that he erred in taking the heat in the 1989 fracas, indicating that not everything that actually transpired that night had come out. Indeed, *Boston Globe* writer and fellow television commentator Will McDonough wrote that Simpson considered the court case to have been one of the biggest mistakes of his life, and that he wished he would have let all the secrets come out at the time. In his own view, it was a minor scuffle, certainly nothing that could be compared with being tackled by a couple of big linebackers on a frozen football field. It was just "a mutual wrestling-type altercation," he had told police.

The second major question—Why would any wife tolerate such treatment beyond the first time she is slapped by her spouse?—is more complicated. Indeed, along with child abuse, it has become one of the leading legal and psychological questions of our day and has been analyzed, theorized, and become the subject of shelves full of pop-psychology books, one of which was written by Nicole's own therapist.

Prior to the Simpson case, the most famous case of wife battering was perhaps that of housewife Francine Hughes. After enduring years of abuse, she was attacked by her husband once again in 1977 and forced to have sex. When he fell asleep, Francine poured gasoline on the bed and set it afire, killing him. She was tried for first-degree murder, but the shocked jury found her not guilty by reason of temporary insanity. The entire nation was jolted when her plight was depicted in a TV movie called *The Burning Bed*.

But wife beating is not new. It is a worldwide problem and crosses all socioeconomic boundaries and has a dreadful pedigree that goes back to the Middle Ages and beyond. Spousal abuse did not appear fully developed like some hot-house flower grown just in America.

Since early Christianity produced most of

the Western world's earliest recorded documents, the Christian Church's writings are held up as a mirror of the civilization of its day, with startling results. Even in the Bible, Ephesians 5:22–23 states that wives should "be subject in everything to their husbands." An 11th-century bishop named Marbode declared women are crafty snares created by the Devil to entrap men, and are both "honey and poison." The word describing men who hate women—misogynist— may be popularly known today, but would seem to fit Bishop Marbode pretty well, too. The Friar Cherubino's "Rules of Marriage" declared that if a husband needs to correct a difficult wife he should "take up a stick and beat her soundly . . . out of charity and concern for her soul."

The French, considered enlightened, decided in the 13th century that the law should not intervene in wife beating "provided he neither kills nor maims her." Napoleon apparently didn't like the direction of everything set forward by the French Revolution and rolled back the laws to leave women without real protection from their husbands. And the Common Law of Wales, showing the English Isles had an eye for legal detail, said it was permissible for a man to punish his wife, but he must use "a rod the length of his forearm and the thickness of his middle finger" and confine the beating to three strokes.

The list goes on and on, making a reader perhaps cringe, but some sense of understanding is impossible without the historical perspective that taught women to be submissive or take a whipping, and to perceive themselves as their husband's property.

A guidebook that is used in the training of police tells of Colonial America adopting a version of the Wales law, declaring that a man has the right "to whip his wife, provided he used a switch no bigger than his thumb." Early Pennsylvania law, however, took dumb statutes a step beyond that, saying that a man could *not* beat his wife after ten o'clock at night or on Sunday.

America changed, but not in everything. As recent as 1974, surveys found that one-fifth of all American men and women approved of slapping one's spouse "on appropriate occasions."

Wife abusers seldom come from well-adjusted families and they come to adulthood as insecure, jealous people. Experts say that although they communicate well in their professional lives, they do not communicate

O.J. Simpson and wife Nicole. (Dominguez/Globe Photos)

Above: San Francisco
49er running back O.J.
Simpson in a 1979 game
against the Los Angeles
Rams. (AP/Lennox
McClendon)

Right: O.J. Simpson the
TV commentator, at
Superbowl XXVII in
January 1993.

Right: O.J. Simpson and girlfriend Paula Barbieri, 1992.

Below: O.J. Simpson appears at the Pediatric AIDS Foundation's "A Time for Heroes" festival in Los Angeles on June 5, 1994. (AP Photo/Donna Gilmartin)

Police tape surrounds the Bundy Drive home of Nicole Brown Simpson following the discovery of the bodies of Nicole and Ronald Goldman. (AP Photo/Eric Draper)

Ronald Goldman in an undated family photo. (AP)

Blood-stained sheets are strewn along the entry-way to Nicole Brown Simpson's home. (AP Photo/Eric Draper)

An unidentified police investigator walks past the blood-stained towels at Nicole Brown Simpson's home. (AP Photo/Eric Draper)

A sign place in the doorway outside the condominium belonging to Nicole Brown Simpson. (Photo/Nick Ut)

A girl looks at signs posted on the gates of the Simpson estate in Brentwood. (AP Photo/Rhonda Birndorf)

O.J. Simpson hangs his head as he sits in his attorney's car, on June 13, 1994, the day after the discovery of the bodies of Nicole Brown Simpson and Ronald Goldman. (AP Photo/Nick Ut)

O.J. Simpson and attorney Howard Weitzman leave police headquarters after Simpson was questioned in connection with the deaths of his ex-wife and Ronald Goldman. (AP Photo/Michael Caulfield)

O.J. Simpson, with daughter Sydney and son Justin, arrives at Nicole's funeral. (AP Photo/Eric Draper)

Cheering O.J. Simpson fans crowd the streets near Simpson's mansion in support of the superstar. (AP Photo/Kevork Djansezian)

Hundreds of onlookers appear outside the condominium of Nicole Brown Simpson. (AP Photo/Michael Caulfield)

Al Cowlings sits at the wheel of his Ford Bronco with Simpson hiding in the back as he leads police on a two-county chase along the freeways of Los Angeles. (AP Photo/Lois Bernstein)

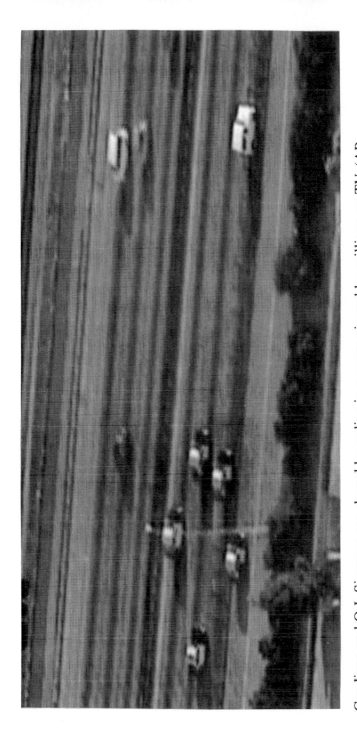

Cowlings and O.J. Simpson are chased by police in a scene viewed by millions on TV. (AP Photo/CNN/KCAL)

Al Cowlings outside the Ford Bronco, its emergency lights blinking, in the driveway of the Simpson mansion during the tense standoff with police. (AP Photo/ABC)

O.J. Simpson is driven to Los Angeles Police Department headquarters following the two-hour freeway chase. (AP Photo/Bob Galbraith)

Al Cowlings following his arrest. (AP Photo/Los Angeles Police Department)

Al Cowlings the day after the two-hour freeway chase. Charged with aiding and abetting a fugitive, he was released on $250,000 bail. (AP Photo/Rhonda Birndorf)

O.J. Simpson with attorney Robert Shapiro at O.J.'s arraignment, June 20, 1994. (AP Photo/Pool, *Los Angeles Times*, Ken Lubas)

O.J. Simpson following his arrest. (AP Photo/Los Angeles Police Department)

very well around their wives, expecting the women to be able to read their minds if something is needed. When she fails to anticipate his needs, the abuser sees that as rejection and explodes.

A man who is an abuser of his wife, according to the pattern, tends to be a model of masculine behavior and therefore expects his wife to be the model of idealized feminine behavior—submissive and subservient. The profile of such a man says that he has a dual personality—brutal at home, but charming, easy-going, and friendly in public. That is why when a particularly savage example of wife abuse is publicized, friends are usually shocked that the husband would even be able to do such a thing. He loved her!

On the other hand, the wives of these men usually possess low self-esteem that dates back to childhood and, in trying to fulfill the stereotyped roles of being perfect wives, mothers, and homemakers, place the needs of everyone else, including physical safety, before their own. They are unable to deal with their anger, saddled with feelings of guilt because they think they are at fault, and as a result are subject to bouts of severe depression.

In Susan Forward's best-selling book, *Men*

Who Hate Women and the Women Who Love Them, the therapist who briefly treated Nicole wrote that the pattern usually begins with a whirlwind courtship that is exciting, sexually powerful, and with a touch of danger. But once the relationship becomes serious, Prince Charming can be transformed into a beast who always has to be in control of every situation, has to win at all costs, on all fronts.

The worshipful wife, early on, rationalized the behavior, believing her man is under a lot of stress, or had too much to drink. Why else would he batter her? Then she makes herself a double victim, first by allowing beatings to continue, then blaming herself for not having done better in dealing with whatever precipitated the problem. Since no one is perfect, she is always doomed to fall short of both of their high expectations.

Money and children are other major factors in such cases.

Through the use of the children, an abusive husband can control his wife. He can threaten to harm them or even take them away from her if she does not obey. The children thus become swept up in the dreadful cycle of seeing Daddy hurt Mommy, hearing them fight, listening to Mommy cry and Daddy yell. Many times, in later life, such scenes will be repeated by the offspring who saw them on a regular basis while growing up, thinking that is the way to handle anger and frustration.

Money is equally important, since the man is usually the breadwinner in such a household. If the woman is ill-trained for earning a living in the outside world, she is terrified of not having financial independence. In the lower economic brackets, that could mean no money for rent or food. In the higher echelons, it means she cannot expect to maintain a lifestyle that may have been hers throughout a long marriage.

Further, the higher up the social scale, the more complex the problem. A woman married to a man of high position is reluctant to break the secrecy of her suffering for fear of ruining her husband's reputation, and through that causing the family to collapse. Such twisted skeins of thought make his problem her fault.

Therefore there are a number of answers to why women stay in such a relationship. Usually, it is a combination of things, from an addictive sort of love, a truly compulsive need for the other person, the fear of losing their children and income, and the wonderful periods of making up after an argument, when roses, chocolates, and kisses replace the slaps and kicks of the night before. He promises it won't happen again, and she believes that he is going to change, and both of them are lying to themselves and to each other. "Nothing bonds a woman to an abuser more addictively than his swings back and forth between love and abuse," Forward wrote.

Police just hate this stuff. Cops know that when they step between a husband and a wife, anything can happen, very little of it logical. And it is very dangerous. FBI statistics have shown that one-fourth of all of the police officers murdered or injured on the job are the result of domestic violence calls. And since wife-beating is such a repetitive crime, the same cops and the same families tend to square off time and again. It extends beyond law enforcement. In Los Angeles, a murder results from domestic violence every nine days. The FBI statistics show that in 1992, a total of 4,936 women were murdered in the nation, and 1,432 of them—29 percent—were killed by boyfriends or husbands.

Even if police successfully intervene, they face what is a truly frustrating situation. Many of the battered wives, even while sniffling in a cop's arms or being hauled to the hospital, will refuse to file charges against the man who brutalized them. Often, police give them both a lecture and leave, knowing that the troubled home will not change.

But even an arrest does not mean the situation is settled. It is not unusual for a husband to post bail within a few hours and return to the house, thinking of revenge. If a divorce is filed, the husband may take to stalking his former domestic partner, jealously ready to strike her or any prospective new man in her life.

Cops say that a battered woman is at the highest point of risk after she leaves her abusive partner, since the husband, who may have been upstanding community member otherwise, has been disgraced in public court and wants to get even. He may start out with the idea that if he could just talk to her about the situation, everything can be resolved, but it almost inevitably escalates to an attack much more severe than anything that had preceded it, triggered by an unreasoning and intense jealousy. The former husband or partner may feel he still has an exclusive claim on her life for all time. The idea that she may become independent and no longer need him at all, or even worse, become involved with another man, is enough to send a habitual abuser over the edge.

The newspapers and television stations covering the bizarre Simpson drama quickly focused on the abuse issue and thrust it into the headlines and kept it there.

Tammy Bruce, president of the Los Angeles chapter of the National Organization for Women, told *Los Angeles Times* reporters that Simpson was apparently far from being unique in such a situation. Instead, she said, he was distressingly typical of husbands who beat their wives. "One thing O.J. kept saying in the police report was, 'This is private business, this is family. I can handle this. This is none of your business.' It's an attitude that runs through the system."

"They're just like anybody else, just regular people. I was stunned by how normal they look," Mary Trinity, the executive director of the Rhode Island Coalition against Domestic Violence, told the *Washington Post*.

"The majority of people who physically assault their spouses are not violent in any other example," observed Murray Strauss, a director of the University of New Hampshire Family Research Laboratory. He told the Associated Press that, "The only difference is that O.J. is publicly known as a nice guy."

So it was against this background that a major part of the Simpson story would unfold. Experts and cops have long since lost their ability to be shocked at finding that a well-known husband, when behind closed doors, bullies and batters his wife. But the general public did not want to believe that O.J. Simpson could have been such a man. Somebody else maybe. A rock star or a politician. Not the Juice!

9

RON AND A.C.

There would be two other major players in the awful drama that was about to unfold in the disturbed lives of Nicole and O.J. Simpson. The role of Ronald Lyle Goldman would be brief, as would his life, while the role of Al Cowlings would be long and complex.

Goldman's mother and father divorced when he was a toddler and while Sharon Rufo remained behind, Fred Goldman moved with his two children from Chicago to the promise of Southern California during its golden years. Later, Fred would marry again and his new wife, Patti, would bring her own three children into the nuclear age brood.

Ron was the eldest and was big brother to the other three boys and one girl in the Goldman household that settled in the Los Angeles suburb of Agoura. As a kid, he played tennis and became so good at the sport that eventually he was paid to give private lessons. He also worked at a hospital for people stricken with cerebral palsy and was a summer camp counselor. But as the good-looking boy grew into a chiseled handsomeness while living in the shadow of Hollywood, he decided that his looks might be his future. By the time he was 25 years old, in 1994, he was living the sort of life that most young Americans probably believe only exists in fanciful television scripts.

The personable Goldman was tall and muscular, living among a bevy of beautiful single girls and a herd of equally handsome guys. All of them, of both sexes, wanted to be models and actors, and it was impossible for anyone but the best, brightest and prettiest to make it into the group. They dressed in casual funk around their neighborhood, because it didn't matter what they wore. They could draw admiring stares, even when walking down the street in worn jeans and oversized shirts.

Ron actually was making real progress in his career, landing a job a model for Giorgio

Armani in a print advertisement and being promised a role in the hunk-and-babe television series *Baywatch*. He had thick black hair that he wore slicked back and parted in the middle, so that it appeared almost like a raven's wings, and he kept the sideburns fashionably short. The angular face had the automatic rugged look about it that the cameras loved, and a strong, square chin. The green eyes were set close together, the Roman nose was arrow-straight and the heavy eyebrows gave him a rather engaging mysterious look. Once asked to rate himself on the usual one-to-ten scale of attractiveness, Ron said he was a "Ten-plus. I'm way up there. There really isn't a scale for me."

He religiously took care of his body, exercising daily, working up a sweat to keep the muscles trim, and watching his diet. Pumping iron, playing softball, or riding a bicycle were as natural as breathing. His crew of friends had no use for drugs and alcohol or long exposure to the California sun, fearing that such things might contaminate the low-fat machines that were their bodies and, horrors, cause a pimple or a wrinkle that could ruin a budding career before the camera and in the fashion pages.

No mistaking it. Ron Goldman looked good strutting in a photo shoot, peeling back a sports jacket and staring down the lens from behind the round, tortoise-shell eyeglasses that he wore when he needed the intelligent look.

In 1992, he got some nationwide television exposure, appearing on a show called *Studs*. He was fit and casually elegant in dark jeans, a blue denim shirt open almost to his navel and a little chain that held a medallion around his neck. Snappy patter went with the gig, and he didn't hesitate when the host asked, "How do you know when it's the right time to make a romantic move?" Ron smacked a right fist into his left palm. "I'm right on it," he said, explaining that he could tell within the first five minutes he spent with a girl whether she was right for him. Apparently, he decided that a lot of them were right for him, because many friends said that Goldman was frequently in the company of beautiful women. "He was a stud, literally," a friend said. In fact, he was living with a girlfriend when he moved to Brentwood in the summer of 1993, but the relationship didn't last.

Part of his charm was that he was a nice guy, always ready to hang out and ever available to help his friends. "He was really sweet. He would sometimes borrow my vacuum cleaner, and when my cat got out he would keep her in his apartment for me," said neighbor Alexandra De Furio. "There wasn't a mean bone in his body," added a softball team chum.

Ron had big plans, big dreams. If the modeling thing didn't work out before he got old, say about 30, he would study to be a paramedic or maybe save up some cash and open his own restaurant. Restaurants are things that the beautiful young of Los Angeles know about, because since there are so many of their throng and so few jobs, most of them end up working, sooner or later, in some sort of eatery in order to pay the rent. For Ron, it was waitering at a trattoria in Brentwood called Mezzaluna, a cozy place with clouds painted on the ceilings, flowers in pots outside the cream-colored walls, and Mexican tiles on the floor.

Life and party seemed to be synonymous for Goldman, and his constant adventuresome spirit attracted people to him. It was not unusual for him to get off work and head out with friends for an entire weekend of hitting one club after another, never really knowing in which of California's beach towns they would end up for breakfast on Monday.

* * *

One morning when Ron and his pals began their day at a local Starbuck's coffee shop, he struck up an acquaintance with a compelling blond woman, obviously older than he but possessing a beauty that captivated everyone who saw her. Nicole Brown Simpson shook his hand with a wary smile, their eyes locked.

Goldman was not a party animal, but also no stranger to such a scene, where lithe, twenty-something girls boogied down and sexuality lay on the floor like a thick carpet. Those, however, were just that—girls. Nicole was a woman! And Ron did a double-take when he learned that she was the ex-wife of none other than O.J. Simpson.

In spite of the differences in their ages, Ron was attracted like a moth to a flame. And the fact that she was the ex-wife of a football legend added element of danger that made their friendship that much tastier, although they were doing nothing wrong.

Soon, Ron Goldman was seen dancing at trendy nightspots with the gorgeous, older fox, playing with her children at the town house on South Bundy, working out with her at a purple-fronted sweat shop called The Gym, taking her along on fashion shoots, and piloting her around in her white

Ferrari convertible with the tan leather seats, a burled wood dash, and the snazzy license plate L84AD8 (Late for a Date). Sexual attractiveness may be the coin of the realm in L.A., but Ron's younger girlfriends didn't have Nicole's kind of money, her style, or the Ferrari, and Ron loved the scene when he would drive her to the front door of some popular dance club in the flash car, turning every head around. "O.J. wouldn't be pleased," he confided to a buddy after one spin in the rakish machine that responded instantly to his slightest touch. "It's his car."

But there were boundaries, and Ron Goldman was smart enough to recognize them. Friends would insist later that Nicole and Ron were just close friends, and police also insisted that there was no history of a romance between the two beautiful people. Close friends insisted that it was all innocent and platonic, primarily because they knew Ron would have never been able to keep such a juicy bit of gossip to himself. If he was having sex with Nicole Simpson, they are sure that he would have told them.

The reason Ron kept his distance was simple. As he told his friends, "If I ever fooled around with Nicole, O.J. would kill me."

* * *

Al Cowlings was O.J. Simpson's shadow, marching through life in lockstep.

They grew up together, they played ball together and to the end, O.J. would remember A.C. as his most trusted and closest friend. No matter what, Simpson always knew that if he turned around, Cowlings' huge presence would be standing there, ready to help, no questions asked.

And why not? Seldom would any two men endure so much together over such a long period of time.

They were kids together back in the early days on Potrero Hill, living in the same housing project, running around, throwing rocks at buses, getting into fights. O.J. was too small to win many fights one-on-one, but the combination of his ability to talk himself out of trouble and the presence of his big buddy standing beside him deterred most challengers. O.J. could talk like a machine gun, something that really impressed Al, who stuttered and had difficulty making himself understood. Wherever O.J. went, A.C. was right behind. Together, they formed the little gang of neighborhood jocks known as the Superiors, which O.J. led and A.C. followed and guarded him. "They were joined at the hip," observed one friend.

That would carry on for years. O.J. made certain throughout his career that Cowlings was given the opportunity to go through doors that may have otherwise been closed to him.

At Galileo High School, on the edge of San Francisco's Chinatown, the coaches who had been thrilled to see what Simpson could do on the football field inherited another gem when O.J. talked A.C. into playing ball. Compared to most of the Asian boys on the team, A.C. was a giant, by far the biggest man on the squad, and by the time he was 16, Cowlings stood 6-foot-3 and weighed 230 pounds.

Simpson went on to play and star at the City College of San Francisco, and Cowlings followed a year later as O.J. encouraged him to keep his grades up. When colleges and universities went nuts trying to recruit O.J., and he finally chose USC, he made certain the following year that the Trojans handed out a scholarship to Al Cowlings, too, who studied criminology. O.J. became an All-American. So did A.C., as part the Trojan defensive team known as the Wild Bunch.

O.J., the first choice in the first draft round, went to the Buffalo Bills. A year later, he prodded the Buffalo management into drafting big and beefy A.C. in the opening round. A defensive end, standing 6-foot-5 and weighing 258 pounds, A.C. was on the other side of the ball, and not specifically a member of The Electric Company. But when the game was over, it was Al back by the side of the Juice. Nobody ever protected O.J. Simpson as well or as long.

Cowlings was traded from the Bills to Houston and then to the Los Angels Rams, but finally caught up with O.J. at the end of their professional careers. They retired at the same time, from the same team, their hometown San Francisco 49ers.

When their football days were over, A.C. moved to Los Angeles to be near his oldest pal, and reaped substantial rewards for doing so. While he worked odd jobs, such as being a bartender, O.J. was getting into many business deals, and A.C.—the one person among his hundreds of friends whom O.J. would trust without thinking—worked with him. When O.J. was shooting a movie and needed a stand-in, there was A.C. to take the fall or make the jump. They were closer than brothers.

There was apparently only one moment of serious dispute in all their years together. When the one university was checking out the football prospects of both Cowlings and Simpson, they allowed the boys to use a rented car for a while. At the time, Cowlings' romance with statuesque Marguerite Whitley was on the rocks, setting the stage for an act straight from Cyrano de Bergerac. The stammering A.C. felt his smooth-talking pal Simpson would be able to express Cowlings' true feelings to Marguerite and he enlisted O.J. to help him iron his problems out. Remarked another friend about that incident, "It was like asking the fox to guard the chicken coop." O.J. put the beautiful girl in the beautiful ca˙ and cruised around San Francisco while A.C. stayed on Potrero Hill, hoping that his buddy's smooth talking would make the girl change her mind. When O.J. promoted himself instead of his buddy and started to date Marguerite, Cowlings became so furious that he tried to turn over the rented car with the new couple still inside of it. O.J. talked Al out of his rage and within the week regained his shadow.

Like most of America, Al Cowlings found it impossible to stay upset with O.J. Simpson. O.J. weaseled his way out of a suspension in school while A.C. took the rap. O.J. stole his best girl and eventually married her.

Cowlings got over such incidents. From following the wisecracking young O.J. around the projects and keeping him out of fights to the final moments of the saga that was about to sweep both of them up into a tragic maelstrom, O.J. Simpson always had one companion to whom he could turn if things went wrong.

Al Cowlings never let him down.

10
MONDAY,
JUNE 13

When the bodies were found sprawled on the blood-soaked tiles beside the gates to Nicole's town house, police immediately remembered that she had a long history of calling the cops during violent arguments with her famous husband. In fact, even long after the divorce became official, O.J. and Nicole were still receiving emergency visits by squad cars at that very condominium complex. Rather than launching a manhunt for some mysterious, unknown killer, the first thing they wanted to know was: Where was O.J.? It took them until dawn to discover that Simpson was not even in Los Angeles, but in a hotel halfway across the country.

Reservations had been made on June 9,

134

nearly a week earlier, to have O.J. take a
red-eye special to Chicago to attend a function being thrown by Hertz. A limousine
delivered him to the Los Angeles International Airport, where he arrived at 11:32
P.M., and boarded American Airlines Flight
668, that took off from LAX at 11:45 P.M.
Since it was the late-night special, Simpson
had the entire first-class section to himself.
He had bumped into one of his many
friends, Howard Bingham, who was on the
same flight. "Hey, Bingham," O.J. had
called out. They talked for a while before
boarding, and then again at the luggage
carousel in Chicago, primarily joking about
O.J.'s golf game. Bingham would later recall
that Simpson seemed at ease and normal,
showing no trace of cuts or blood. "Nothing
seemed different about him. . . . He seemed
like always," Bingham told *The Boston
Globe*.

The plane landed in Chicago at 5:34 on
Monday morning.

He went directly to the O'Hare Plaza-
Hotel, a blocky, sand-colored building near
the busy Chicago airport, and checked in at
6:15 A.M., tired after the all-night flight. But
ever ready to please the fans, he took some
time to sign autographs and chat with the
front desk clerk. He asked that he not be

disturbed for the next few hours while he slept, then took the elevator to the ninth floor of the eleven-story building, telling the bellman carrying his luggage that he was looking forward to playing some golf while he was there. They found the door bearing a brass plaque with the numbers 915, slid the plastic key card into the lock, and O.J. retired for a quick few hours of rest.

That is where a Los Angeles police officer's telephone call reached him to advise that his ex-wife and a male friend had been murdered, and that the police wanted him to return home immediately. Simpson made a series of telephone calls, including one to his lawyer Howard Weitzman in California, and then rushed downstairs, where he played the celebrity card to cut into a line of people waiting at the checkout counter and had the hotel order him a taxi immediately. He left the hotel in time to make American Airlines Flight 1691, which left Chicago at 7:41 A.M. Central Time. The airplane touched down back at LAX, returning O.J. to Los Angeles, at 11:08 A.M. Pacific Time, and an exhausted Simpson got into a friend's shining black Mercedes for the twelve-mile drive home to the mansion on Rockingham Drive.

Twenty-two minutes later, the car pulled

up at the entrance to his cobblestone driveway and O.J., wearing black pants and a
white polo shirt, got out, threw the strap of
his carry-on luggage over his left shoulder,
and walked toward the ornate wrought-iron
green gate that opened onto his mansion's
immaculate grounds. Three police officers
were standing there, talking, when the car
arrived. Quickly they peeled away and surrounded him, both to escort him to the
house and shield him from the media. A
small female officer reached behind her and
produced a pair of handcuffs that were soon
clipped to his wrists and a large black cop
took a firm grip on O.J.'s arm. The genuine
American hero could then be seen beneath
the trees on his lush estate, with his arms
manacled behind his back.

A very strange event then took place. At
noon, escorted by his lawyer, Howard L.
Weitzman, O.J. Simpson, was driven by police to their Parker Center headquarters for
questioning. The handcuffs had been removed, but there was no doubt that Simpson was, in football parlance, "in the grasp"
of the police.

Over the next three and a half hours,
Simpson was questioned and searched by
police, and reports claimed they found

scratches on his body and a slice on his hand.

Trying to reconstruct his movements, they learned that on Saturday night, he had escorted beautiful, dark-haired model Paula Barbieri, whom he had been dating regularly, to a $25,000 per couple fund-raiser, a black-tie affair in nearby Bel Air. People at the party would tell police that O.J. seemed perfectly normal, his usual gracious self, during the evening.

Sunday, he played golf at the Riviera Country Club a few blocks from his home early in the day with one of his regular partners, a man who would later say Simpson appeared to be fine. But Mitchell Mesko, who was O.J.'s caddy for the round, would come forward to say the Juice angrily blew up when his golfing partner made an off-hand joke and even threatened to beat up the man. Mesko, in giving his story to the TV tabloid *A Current Affair*, told that O.J., ashamed of the outburst, said, "Mitch, I'm a pathetic person." The caddy replied, "Juice, you're not a pathetic person. You're a pathetic golfer."

The police then listened as O.J. described how he and Nicole had attended a dance recital for their daughter at Paul Revere Middle School on Sunday afternoon, and that they parted amiably at 6 o'clock. Nicole went directly to Mezzaluna's with a group of seven others, including her kids. O.J. was not among them.

When the long interview was done, police had a laundry list of things they could begin checking. When O.J. left the police station, he moved slowly and zombielike, without direction or emotion, his trademark smile was gone, replaced by a somber, blank look, and he waded through the herd of stalking photographers and reporters as if astonished at their presence.

Weitzman decided it was time to break the media silence on the investigation. He said that O.J. had been at "a function with the family and kids and apparently everything was fine" on Sunday evening when he had last seen his ex-wife.

"Mr. Simpson was advised of this tragedy in Chicago and flew back immediately," Weitzman told the reporters, adding that O.J. probably was on his way to the Los Angeles airport, or already there, when the deaths occurred. His client was "absolutely shocked and upset" at the tragic death of Nicole, the lawyer said, because the couple had been "getting along on a more cordial basis."

"I am convinced that he is innocent," said Weitzman.

So what could be wrong with this picture? Weitzman, after all, was an attorney that was rated by the *Martindale-Hubbell Law Directory* to be among the preeminent people in the legal profession. A 54-year-old UCLA graduate with almost thirty years at the bar, he was a partner in the Century Plaza law firm of Katten Muchin Zavis & Weitzman and had waged high-profile legal battles on behalf of such luminaries as automaker John DeLorean, getting him off on cocaine charges in one celebrated case. Other clients included actress Kim Basinger, heavyweight boxing champion Mike Tyson, and another superstar, singer Michael Jackson. Although small in stature, Weitzman is huge in reputation, and favors meeting all charges with a blistering counterattack.

Chris Rush, one of the nation's top private investigators, pointed out the discrepancy of what had just happened with O.J. Simpson. The police, despite their searches of the town house and Simpson's mansion, were not yet ready to bring formal charges against anybody for anything. Indeed, LAPD Commander David Gascon emphasized to reporters that police "will be interviewing everyone even remotely associated with this case, and that would include any other potential witnesses. I would hasten to add that everyone is a witness at this point, no one has been arrested, no one has been charged."

According to Rush, the proper procedure in a case that would have to be based solely on circumstantial evidence is to have a client say nothing at all. "The lawyer should have said, 'Charge him or we're out of here,' " said Rush.

Instead, Simpson was allowed to talk with the police for three and a half hours, which allowed them to get information on the record on specific times, places, and actions. Once they had that information, there was no wiggle room left in the excuse box. He had given them something to investigate when all he really had to do was remain silent, as was his right under the Constitution. It would not be the last time a Simpson lawyer made a decision that other professionals might consider peculiar.

Police were delighted to get the information, for all they had at the moment were scraps of evidence. Still, aware of the celebrity status of the case, they played their public cards carefully. "Mr. Simpson has been taken in as a possible witness, which is routine in any form of homicide," Gascon said, not bothering to explain whether locking him in handcuffs, even if for such a brief time, was standard for someone who was, at that point, not charged with so much as spitting on the sidewalk.

In another unexpected move, District Attorney Gil Garcetti assigned the case to one of his most highly regarded prosecutors, Marcia Clark of the special trials section. No arrest had been made, but an assistant district attorney was already getting ready for trial.

Weitzman drove O.J. home and the grief-stricken Simpson came through the ever-growing crowd outside with his face down, shielding his eyes from the prying cameras. He would spend the night elsewhere, although friends and family members had poured into the mansion to lend him support as soon as the word of the tragedy spread. Former teammate Bob Chandler told reporters it was "obviously a tragic situation. We're just hoping for the best of everything." Paul McGuire, an NBC announcer who worked football games with O.J., expressed the dismay in which his closest friends suddenly found themselves. "You've got to be sick to your stomach because you know him and you wonder how you can help him. I mean, what can you do? I know he's hurting."

The police clearly had evidence that made them feel they had a strong advantage in this contest. Ever since the bodies had been discovered, the investigative apparatus had been in high gear, and they found enough straws to make a small haystack.

Not only was there blood all over the steps where the bodies of Nicole and Goldman were discovered, but suspicious reddish-brown spots had been found on the cobblestones of Simpson's driveway, some twenty yards from his garage. Investigators folded little tents of cardboard over each spot so forensic specialists could take samples of the blotches, which turned out to be blood. Blood was reportedly discovered in the white Ford Bronco, rented to O.J. by Hertz, and parked in the driveway. The vehicle was towed away, rear wheels off the ground, and impounded as evidence.

They sent detectives around to Mezzaluna and to talk to Goldman's friends to determine what had been his relationship with Nicole. Later, they announced that the two were not romantically involved. Joy Ploussard, a co-worker at the restaurant, said her friend apparently was killed because he happened to be "in the wrong place at the wrong time."

John DeBello, the restaurant's manager, had a rueful comment, recalling that the last time he had seen Goldman alive, he warned Ron not to take those sunglasses back at that time of night. "I told him he shouldn't go. With someone of that caliber, it doesn't look good," DeBello said. Perhaps if Goldman had listened to his friend's advice, he would not have become a victim that night.

Specialists who arrived at the town house in a boxy, black van that bore the sign CRIMINALISTICS LABORATORY worked the area on their hands and knees in a search for evidence. They found a bloody glove in the bushes and dropped it into an evidence bag. The sun overhead kept much of their work dappled in shadows as they knelt on the blood-stained sheets that had once covered the bodies, and picked at cracks and crevices in their minute search for evidence.

The more they found, the greater their suspicions grew, although they kept things under tight wraps. O.J. had already given the police his statement, and now they were chewing away at the edges of the story.

One weapon they had was the press. Careful leaks to certain reporters had the effect of sending shock waves to Simpson and his legal advisers. Although police officials sternly stood up to deny what was happening, sometimes reporters actually knew within minutes some of the findings that had been discussed in a so-called confidential meeting at police headquarters. Anyone familiar with the practice of leaking information to obtain a reaction was aware of what was happening.

"They're doing it to make him rabbit," said Chris Rush. "They can't bring him in and toast him anymore without a charge, but they can make him nervous."

From Chicago came word that police in the Windy City had checked the hotel room where O.J. had stayed briefly Monday morning and that they had discovered a bloody towel and a broken glass. In Los Angeles, Simpson's lawyer said his client was so upset upon hearing the news of Nicole's death that he slammed his hand down in anger, breaking a glass and cutting a finger.

Police also turned some light on the 1989 beating incident in which O.J. was arrested, and the results clearly put O.J. into the murky spotlight of a possible suspect. Police sealed the 911 emergency call from that incident, and all other such calls she had made. But they confirmed that officers had been called to the town house by Nicole several times since January because of disturbances.

Police worked feverishly, measuring the time and distance between O.J.'s mansion and the airport and beginning the time consuming process of establishing a DNA profile on the blood samples that had been recovered. While it is a simple matter to determine the type of blood, a DNA test takes longer and has better use in court. If a DNA match is made between samples, there is almost 100 percent certainty that it is accurate. The district attorney wished to take no chances in the effort to prove or disprove whether O.J.'s blood was in evidence at the crime scene, or if a drop of Nicole's or Goldman's blood had been found at O.J.'s home.

By the end of the day, the cops and scientists and prosecution lawyers felt they had already found a great deal of evidence that pointed directly to O.J. Simpson. But they could not yet grab him. A wrongful arrest of one of the most recognizable and popular black men in the nation could set Los Angeles ablaze again.

That did not mean officials could not tighten the net a little more, give O.J. and his lawyer another squeeze. On Tuesday morning, the *Los Angeles Times* story on the murder investigation declared that sources close to the investigation said the evidence was mounting and that O.J. Simpson might be arrested within a few days.

As the sun went down, a small shrine of flowers and notes had already begun to take shape at the doorway to Nicole's condominium. In all the furor surrounding the star of the drama and the national outpouring of shock over the murders and sympathy for O.J., people were also remembering that a woman and a young man, both of them so attractive that even their driver's license pictures seem to be fashion portraits, had died in a brutal and savage attack, and that two little children were caught in a whirlwind that was destroying their family. Bundles of carnations and other flowers were laid on the tile pathway, and notes were taped to the wall. One, meant for the Simpson children, read, "Mothers hold their children's hands for a short while—their hearts forever. God bless you both and may your mother's spirit reside in your heart forever." It was signed by "Adam and Ali and their Mom."

Another termed Nicole to be The White Light and The World's Best Mom. "You gave your children so much love it will carry them through 100 lives," it said.

The murders of Nicole Brown Simpson and Ronald Lyle Goldman, with none other than O.J. Simpson himself being the prime suspect, created a few ulcers in those who labored in the Los Angeles Police Department and in the office of District Attorney Gil Garcetti. Just what the city did not need at this moment in its checkered history was a monster of a celebrity case. Few people would have been surprised if Garcetti, a slim and dapper man who had been in office only eighteen months but had served twenty-five years in the department as an assistant district attorney, should have suddenly declared he had decided to retire and move to somewhere nice and quiet, like war-scarred Bosnia or bloody little Rwanda.

For if one thing was certain, it was that the law enforcement apparatus of Los Angeles was once again about to be put under the microscope.

The long nightmare had begun for the cops and prosecutors with the 1991 police beating of motorist Rodney G. King, a black man. Not only had the brutal assault been captured on videotape and played thousands of times around America, making the

L.A. cops look like a bunch of hooligans, but the resulting trial of the accused officers ended with the city being engulfed by riots that spawned another round of trials and controversy. The bottom line in the King case and the riots was that the police had not done their jobs very well, and controversial Chief Darryl Gates was replaced by a progressive black, Willie L. Williams. Things would change, promised Williams.

Then the district attorney's office was handed a major embarrassment, also seen by millions on television, when its prosecutors—armed with a confession—blew the first murder trial of Lyle and Erik Menendez, the rich kids who admitted killing their parents in a shotgun barrage. The D.A. team may have thought the case was a slam dunk for conviction, but they soon learned that they were wrong. An aggressive defense team turned the case on its head, accused the parents of sexual abuse, and actually persuaded enough jurors to believe their claim that the shootings were really acts of self defense. Millions of people around the nation had watched the trial unfold on television, day after day, like a soap opera. The juries became stuck and could not reach a verdict on anything, and the whole scene was ordered back to the starting line for a new trial. The bottom line in the Menendez case was that the city's prosecutors had not done their jobs very well. Controversial District Attorney Chief Ira Reiner was replaced by Gil Garcetti, who also promised things would change.

For both Williams and Garcetti, it was time to put up or shut up. The media was on the Simpson case like a pack of hungry hounds on the trail of a rabbit. The cops and prosecutors knew their every single move would be watched and analyzed. If any mistakes were made, even minor ones, they again would take a battering from the public.

They didn't know the half of it. The O.J. Simpson case would turn out to be something that none of them—or anyone else— ever had seen, or even could have envisioned. And a rivalry surfaced immediately as the street cops wanted the D.A. to move fast on Simpson, while Garcetti's people chose the methodical, careful route. It drove a wedge into the investigative team and produced an unusual amount of information leaks from cops who wanted to push the D.A.'s office into action.

11

Tuesday, June 14

The autopsies on Nicole Brown Simpson and Ronald Lyle Goldman were completed on Tuesday and confirmed that a terrible struggle had taken place. Nicole's beautiful cheeks were scraped raw and Goldman's massive wounds were consistent with the idea that the bodybuilder had not been quickly overpowered by his attacker. Nicole's throat was slit to the spinal column, nearly decapitating her, and Goldman's body bore twenty-two puncture wounds, including a throat cut. Both died, said the coroner, of "multiple sharp-force injuries and stab wounds." In other words, the murder weapon was a knife.

The news media was already reporting, firmly, that police sources were saying that

O.J. Simpson was the prime suspect in the case. The leaks had begun already beginning.

The police, however, still were stuck with only circumstantial evidence. They had no eyewitnesses to the murders, and therefore had to build a case on what little forensic evidence they could find, such as measuring the drive to Los Angeles International Airport. They found that the timeline might be tight, but it could work on a Sunday night with little traffic. Someone could have been in Brentwood at the time of the slayings and still have made it to LAX in time for that American Airlines red-eye flight to Chicago.

One solid piece of evidence was discovered in the bushes beside the fallen bodies. A detective carefully picked up a blood-stained man's work glove and dropped it into a brown paper evidence bag, and that was followed by an unnamed source telling the *Los Angeles Daily News* that a similar glove, also soaked with blood, had been found in O.J.'s mansion.

That was enough to bring Weitzman, the attorney, back to the microphones to deny flatly that assertion, which if allowed to stand unchallenged would indicate a direct link between the murder scene two miles away and the mansion.

"Not only is he going through a tremendous grieving period, but all these rumors about his possible involvement are circulating," Weitzman added. "He came back here, cooperated, and has not been officially told he cannot leave or that he is a suspect. But he has to sit here and listen to all these rumors. . . . It really is a horrible time for O.J."

"It's difficult enough with the shock that your wife's been murdered, but to hear that you may be accused of it, well, it's awful," the lawyer declared. "I am convinced he is innocent."

The beautiful estate behind the green wrought-iron gate that blocked the cobblestone drive remained almost tranquil, as friends and family parked their cars near O.J.'s Bentley and went directly inside. Exiting, they tried to avoid reporters.

That was becoming impossible and would prove even more so as the media circus outside the gate began to shift into high gear. The once-quiet street was lined by television trucks with satellite dishes scooping toward the sky, and stations all over the nation rushed a reporter to Brentwood for on-the-spot reports. At night, their bright lights would give an eerie glow to the street, and by day, dozens upon dozens of well-coiffed television reporters stood in lines, microphones in hand and the mansion in the background, to deliver their reports, most of which had been gleaned from the morning's newspaper columns. Women reporters primped and men even ducked down to use side mirrors on the vans so they could lather up and shave before going on the air to the folks back home. As the hours wore on, more and more newspaper reporters and photographers and television sound engineers, producers, cameramen, and reporters flocked to the scene, as did curious passersby drifting through for a glimpse of the action. A medieval carnival atmosphere reigned, as the street beyond O.J.'s home became an unmanageable zoo, something enjoyed only by the pizza delivery people who were constantly buzzed on cellular news phones to bring over food to the crews who refused to leave the scene. Anything that moved was going to be photographed and questioned, for a hungry public was snapping up every morsel of information and clamoring for more. There was no more popular coffee time topic Tuesday morning than the drama that was unfolding in Brentwood. A stunned public hotly defended their hero and sympathized with his tragic loss.

O.J. did not appear.

But leaks continued to spring from the porous police department, including a new twist to the growing tale of problems encountered after Simpson's divorce. A source told the *Los Angeles Times* that Nicole had informed O.J. several weeks prior to her death that there would be no reconciliation with him. At the same time, police confirmed for the press that they had been frequently summoned to the townhouse in the past months. It was a Chinese water torturous method of letting the suspect know that he was not in custody, but neither had he been forgotten by the people who carry badges.

Still no charges were brought. Only the incessant drumbeat of rumors fed by unnamed sources painted black borders around the heretofore unblemished photo of O.J. Simpson, everybody's hero. If ever O.J. had felt like the opposition was piling on top of him, crushing him, it would have been this day. And it looked as if was only going to get worse.

In Chicago, the staff of the O'Hare Plaza-Hotel confirmed that when O.J. received the call from the police in Los Angeles, the only one he got that morning, he immediately made about ten of his own from the small telephone on his bedside table. Then he hurried downstairs to the lobby, checked out, and forced his way into a line of guests waiting for cabs.

Unexpectedly, the spousal abuse issue was ignited in full flare when Susan Forward, Nicole's former therapist, was interviewed by KCBS-TV. Psychotherapists normally maintain a strict confidentiality on what patients disclose to them. Indeed, in the Menendez case, it took prosecutors three years of legal wrangling before a therapist was allowed to testify about the confession the two boys gave, detailing how they killed their mother and father. Things can move fast in Los Angeles, however, particularly when microphones are placed before people. Forward said that since Nicole was dead, confidentiality no longer applied, and that Nicole had confided to her that she lived in constant fear of being beaten by O.J. Forward said the stalking ex-husband had threatened to kill Nicole, claiming that if he could not have her, then no one could.

An attorney for O.J.'s first wife, when contacted by the media, sidestepped the matter, saying only that abuse was not raised as an issue in the formal divorce proceedings.

Despite it all, the people who had known O.J. during his many years of starring in the sports and entertainment worlds were in a state of total disbelief that something as awful as a double murder could be laid at his doorstep. "I love O.J.," said Jim Lampley, the host of *NFL Live* on NBC and a pal of Simpson's for two decades. "I'm 1,000 percent confident he won't be charged. My thoughts and prayers are with O.J. and his entire family at this terrible time of loss."

"This is bizarre, almost incomprehensible," said Al Michaels, the indefatigable ABC-TV sports anchor. Will McDonough added that, "At NBC, if you ever took a vote on the most popular guy, O.J. would win by a landslide." Terry O'Neill, a close friend of Simpson's and a television producer, summed up the hard line that most of Juice's friends, shaken by the impossibility of such an idol falling so hard, were taking. "In a million years, I will not believe O.J. had anything to do with this," he told *USA Today*. "I don't care what the judicial outcome is. I can never imagine the O.J. that I know doing this."

Doubts were beginning to pop up elsewhere, like unwelcome weeds after a spring rain. Over at Hertz, conversations about the O.J. dilemma ran rampant, for since 1975 the rental-car agency had been tied to the fast-moving coattails of O.J. Simpson. The question was: What does a huge corporation, which spends millions on advertising, do with a closet full of high-priced commercials featuring a man who suddenly was under a black cloud of suspicion? Already the calls were coming in from reporters wanting to know what the company was going to do. For the moment the answer was to sit tight, do nothing, and hope for the best.

In Los Angeles, as police carefully looked for anything remotely resembling evidence, O.J. remained at the mansion, huddling for 15 minutes with his lawyer and talking to friends who described him as totally distraught.

And from what the friends were saying, O.J. stuck by his story that he didn't do it. No matter how the forensic evidence was shaping up, no matter that the damning leaks kept springing out of unnamed police sources, Juice did not waver. Through his shock and grief, Simpson steadily maintained that he had nothing to do with the death of his wife.

The result was that, once again, the law enforcement agencies were having to walk on eggshells. If a street person, or someone other than a megacelebrity of O.J. Simpson's status, had been suspected of a double murder, police would have already moved for an arrest and the D.A. could have decided that the investigators had come up with enough evidence to support an arrest.

But not now. Not when all of the cameras and reporters were standing outside those green gates, ready to pounce on any inconsistency and broadcast the results into the homes of millions of people. When they finally moved, the prosecutors wanted to be absolutely, 100 percent certain that there was plenty of supportive evidence, so O.J. would not be able to slip through their fingers. So they raised the threshold for an arrest, although couching their reticence behind a mask of just being thorough with the investigation. Already, O.J.'s fame and glory were buying him special treatment in the eyes of the law.

12

WEDNESDAY,
JUNE 15

For the news media, the double homicide had happened at the worst possible time. Newsrooms are empty at midnight on Sunday. Television stations are into *Gilligan's Island* reruns by then and newspapers have published the fat Sunday papers and the big-league reporters are home asleep, getting ready for another week. Monday papers are slim because nothing happens on weekends, and it was too late to get anything into the Monday morning papers anyway. Since TV and radio news feed off of newspaper headlines, they have even less to do. In other words, nobody was ready for what was happening in the early Monday hours.

The rapidly changing story remained confusing throughout Monday, and did not make much of a national ripple on the evening news or even in the Tuesday morning papers. The *Los Angeles Times*, as could be expected, had a solid story on Tuesday, putting it on Page 1-A beneath the one-column headline of "O.J. Simpson's Ex-Wife, Man Found Slain." The *New York Times* published a short, almost dismissive story beneath the headline "Ex-Wife of O.J. Simpson Is Slain Outside Her Los Angeles Condo." With the biggest newspapers on each coast on top of the story, it took off.

The media finally caught up with the story on Wednesday morning and would gnaw at it furiously for the rest of the week, making up for lost time. For by Wednesday, the discovery of the bodies and O.J.'s return were combined with the ongoing police news leaks and the gathering of evidence to allow the headlines to shout: Clues Point to Simpson. The circus was on, and who could blame the media for stampeding to this one? The American public was already transfixed by the story and the interest was only going to grow.

The still-anonymous Los Angeles police sources told reporters that day that some of the blood spilled at Nicole's home matched O.J. Simpson's blood type. All that scraping of the rust-colored spots, the serology tests, had paid off handsomely for the cops, who were now throwing some pretty sharp darts in the direction of the superstar. Although many people share any specific blood type, the presence of a type of blood that did not match that of either victim was a significant find. And that O.J. had that very blood type was considered a breakthrough in the investigation. Work continued on the more specific DNA blood workups, but the results could take weeks.

Cop leaks also added fuel to the controversy over the gloves. Weitzman had firmly denied that a second glove was found on O.J.'s property, and the sources within the police department countered not with a news conference but with carefully planted information designed to do maximum damage to the suspect's credibility. They said another work glove had indeed been discovered, and to make the point, added that it was picked up near a side entrance to the mansion grounds, close to a series of spots that had been found to be drops of blood. Weitzman could not back down in public, so he waltzed around the issue. "That would be inconsistent with what I was told" by a police official, he said. "Beyond that, I have no comment."

Then he quit the case.

* * *

It was tantamount to throwing a match under a can of gasoline, and the expected explosion of confusion further heightened the interest of millions of people now keeping track of the unfolding drama.

Weitzman had been called by O.J. from his Chicago hotel room three days before and, from that moment, unwaveringly had defended Simpson's proclaimed innocence. Of course, he also allowed O.J. to be grilled by police for several hours without his client being formally charged with anything. "I've decided because of my personal relationship with O.J. Simpson and my many other professional commitments I can no longer give O.J. the attention he both deserves and needs," said Weitzman. "I will continue to advise and consult with O.J. and provide whatever support I can."

Exit Weitzman, stage left. Enter, stage right, Robert Shapiro. O.J., still not accused officially of anything, was already on his second celebrity lawyer in three days.

Shapiro's client list included baseball players Daryl Strawberry with his drug problem, Vince Coleman, who was nailed for throwing a firecracker at a group of fans, and frequently troubled Jose Canseco; singer Tina Sinatra, and Christian Brando, the son of actor Marlon Brando. He had been Michael Jackson's lead lawyer until ten months previously when he was replaced in that position by Weitzman. And adding to the almost comical merry-go-round that is ridden by Hollywood's top defense lawyers, Shapiro had been the lawyer who coaxed Erik Menendez back from Israel to surrender to Los Angeles police before stepping down in that case, to be replaced by Leslie Abramson, the fiery attorney who turned the Menendez trial inside out.

So the game of legal tennis in the Simpson matter continued with Shapiro, in shirt sleeves, now at the microphone in front of the police headquarters, putting his own spin on the story. Simpson was "extremely depressed" and being treated by a doctor "to help him in this time of grieving.

"He is going to be in seclusion with his family to grieve over the loss of the mother of his children," the lawyer said. Inside the mansion, Shapiro instructed his new client to keep the television set turned off and forego reading newspapers.

Then Shapiro demonstrated why lawyers perhaps should not be so eager to talk to the press before their client is charged. The attorney, who is very good at answering questions in a precise and calm manner, declared, "At the time this murder took place, O.J. was at home waiting to get into a limousine to take him to the airport on a trip that had been planned well in advance for a promotional trip to Chicago."

Weitzman had waffled on the issue, saying that O.J. was on his way to the airport or already there when the murders happened. That was a general statement, particularly since an official time of death had not been established. But Shapiro was firm in his assertion. By announcing that information, Shapiro not only challenged Weitzman's earlier statement, but provided Simpson with an alibi, and police immediately set out to test how well it held up. If it was shaky, O.J. might be forced to change his story again. Simpson's attorneys were backing their client into a corner. The press, although hungry for information, actually would have been just as happy if a public relations specialist had been sent out to say something like the deaths were horrible, O.J. was innocent, and a formal statement would be issued when things settled down in the next few days.

Police were playing the game better, keeping mum officially and feigning outrage at the inside tips being fed to reporters. "I certainly have no intention of labeling him one way or the other," Commander David Gascon said. Then the inside scoop being spoonfed to some reporters, under the condition that the sources' names not be used, led Los Angeles newspapers to keep the heat on O.J. and the defense, and by reverse pressure, also on the prosecutors and their turtlelike pace. The stories stated repeatedly that police considered him now to be their prime suspect, an elevation from the original description of him being just another possible witness.

One vital part of the puzzle was still missing. Neither the unnamed sources nor Simpson's lawyers were accounting for his movements during the hours after he left Nicole at the dance recital around 6 P.M. on Sunday.

Wednesday was also a day of mourning for the victims' families.

In suburban Agoura, the Goldman family stepped out of their seclusion to gather around a huge bank of microphones placed in the red-brick driveway before their home to eulogize Ron. Arms linked, tears flowing, and surrounded by reporters, cameras on tripods and microphones on sound booms that were lowered over their heads, they became part of the day's newsfilm.

"I guess the bottom line is that Ron was a good person from the top of his head to the bottom of his feet, from the inside to the outside," his father, Fred Goldman, said in a voice choked with emotion. "He was a special human being. He didn't deserve what's happened."

Police, Goldman said, had not been helpful in discussing what had happened to their son, telling them they would talk about it later when things settled down.

Fred Goldman said his son "liked to be out and about" with people, but the image being drawn by the media of some kid living in the fast lane were erroneous. He had a lot of friends, a lot of women friends, and Nicole Simpson was just one of them. There had been no hanky-panky going on between them.

"I don't want to get into the innuendoes, rumors, the monkey business going around for Ron's sake and for Nicole's sake. He was very open with us about the women he dated. If Ron was anything more than a friend we would have known," Goldman said.

The emotional father also said it did not surprise anyone in the family that Ron would have volunteered to return the sunglasses to his friend. "And if any of the few little things we've heard of Ron putting up quite a fight . . . that wouldn't surprise me, either." He would not comment when reporters asked how he felt about O.J. Simpson. He kept focused on his son, and the saddest comment had to do with the age at which the young man had perished, how a bright future had been wiped out by a nameless villian. "He loved people," the father said, tears streaming down his cheeks. "He was just getting his life together."

Nicole Brown Simpson was also mourned that day by members of her family, including her ex-husband. It was a private affair at the O'Connor Laguna Hills Mortuary, but nothing could be truly private at times like these.

A pair of black limousines with heavily tinted windows had left the Brentwood estate, destination unknown to the press, but the media had staked out the funeral home, too. O.J. walked solemnly up the steps and spent about two hours at the memorial service. A television camera was waiting for him as he exited, and the latest media invasion of the family's privacy drew anger from Nicole's sister, Denise Brown. "We had a viewing . . . to send my sister off," she said. "We all went and paid our respects. Yes, O.J. was there. But what's the big deal? It's his ex-wife. My God, it's somebody we all love. We just want to let her go in peace." There was no distress among the Brown family that O.J. showed up. Like Fred Goldman, Denise Brown said if the family was upset with anyone, it was the intrusive media herd and the authorities in charge of the case who would tell them little about the death of Nicole.

As quickly as he had been spotted by the video paparazzi, O.J. dropped out of sight again, heading for the Orange County home of his former in-laws, who had taken over the care of his children, shielding them from the news reports. He spent some time with his daughter and son, then returned home, once again having to drive through the gauntlet of reporters and photographers who had assembled outside the gate like some brightly lit horde of well-dressed barbarians laying siege to a castle. As much as the people close to him may have wished, the press wasn't about to go away. The police smiled. Having the place surrounded by the media was like having hundreds of extra eyes keeping track of exactly where O.J. was at all times. They erected platforms, climbed ladders along the walls, and had helicopters clattering in the sky overhead. Neighbors along Rockingham Avenue, particularly at the dead-end intersection of Ashford Street where the Simpson mansion was located, were growing exasperated with the media invasion that showed no sign of letting up.

The cops, however, liked having the press right where it was. They smugly thought that nobody could slip through that sort of net, forgetting at a vital juncture of the case that they were dealing with a man who had defied legions of talented football players during an all-star career.

In New York, famed defense lawyer William Kuntsler said that the press was simply being used, played like a violin by the cops. "It isn't the media's fault that this feeding frenzy has occurred. It's the police who have generated it," he said.

Both sides of the case were also looking ahead to a very peculiar possibility, one that has rarely come up in a criminal case. Sometimes, when a crime is well-publicized, a judge will grant a change of venue, allowing the trial to be held outside of the area where it occurred to have a better chance of getting an impartial jury. It was now clear that even if O.J. were arrested and put on trial, the job of finding a dozen jurors who didn't already know everything about the allegations against him would be extraordinarily difficult. The prosecution might be able to move it away from downtown Los Angeles, but how do you find an impartial jury in a case involving a superstar where every detail was being gobbled up nationwide. San Diego? Arizona? Iowa? Florida? Television had pulled America together into a global community and now people everywhere were forming opinions before O.J. was even formally accused.

O.J.'s friends were sticking by him, but their tone was changing. Singer Dionne Warwick told the media, while she was driving through the gate, that she was only going to tell O.J., "I'm here for you if you need me." Neighbor and TV consumer reporter David Horowitz described O.J. as "a folk hero" who was liked not only worldwide but also within the neighborhood, which was "devastated" by the mystery. But Horowitz said that neighbors were coming to acknowledge "the sad fact that he may have been involved. Did he do it? Everyone is speculating. Did he do it?" Not exactly ringing endorsements from close friends.

13

Thursday, June 16

The whole thing began to unravel like a ball of string on June 16, and the first signs that the façade was beginning to crack surfaced at the funerals for Nicole and Ron.

A white limousine delivered O.J. to the services for Nicole. He wore a tailored black suit, dark glasses to hide his sunken, distraught eyes, and he was flanked by security guards. As the broken family stood beside the casket, O.J. kissed his kids and held their hands before taking them into a side entrance of the church. Sydney Brooke and Justin looked dazed, as if they were not able to comprehend that their mother was gone. How could they possibly understand the enormity of what was happening to them? Uncomprehending, their ears picked up the

172

soft voice of their father, the murmur of mourners, and the overhead clatter of press helicopters whirling about the sunny sky like large, uncaring mosquitoes.

Simpson did not speak at the funeral that took place at St. Martin of Tours Roman Catholic Church in Brentwood. A bevy of close friends and famous athletes, including Olympic champion Bruce Jenner, attended, and heard Nicole's sister eulogize her as "a great mom and a great friend." Howard Weitzman, the expelled lawyer, attended and Simpson's mother, Eunice, wrapped him in an embrace, saying, "Do everything you can for O.J. The children need their father." O.J. wept.

Steve Garvey, a former baseball star who had fallen afoul of the media himself in a couple of paternity actions, described it as "a beautiful eulogy for a beautiful woman and mother."

The coffin was then placed in a white hearse for the trip to the Ascension Cemetery in Lake Forest, some fifty miles to the south. Naturally, they arranged for tight security. With a few hundred members of the press corralled across the street, no one wanted any of them to barge into the church and further darken an already sad day. Even the priest had to show his identification before he was allowed to enter the grounds of the cemetery to conduct the graveside services. Making sure that O.J. was protected, as always, was Al Cowlings, who stood sentinel, dressed in a somber black suit and white tie, almost the identical outfit that O.J. wore. That was not a coincidence, and would soon play an unexpectedly important part in the story.

Ron Goldman was laid to rest in a flower-decked white casket at the Valley Oaks Memorial Park near the home of his father and family in Agoura Hills. His mother, who had not seen him for years, and not had any contact for three years, flew in from St. Louis for the services. His 22-year-old sister, Kim, in tears, eulogized him in services at a tiny chapel in Westlake Village. "Not in my worst nightmare did I imagine that I would be here in front of our family and friends saying how much I'll miss you. I admire everything about you. I don't know if I ever told you how proud I am of the man you have become."

Any sympathy that Ron's friends may still have harbored for O.J. was wearing thin, and anger was not far below the surface for the approximately four hundred friends who gathered at the chapel, many of them having to stand outside because of the over-flow condition. The services were broadcast to them by loudspeakers. "I want O.J. to turn himself in," said a friend of the family. "O.J., if you turn yourself in, at least your children would have some money because you are going to spend all of your money on court cases and you are going to lose."

Police remained officially silent. L.A. Police Chief Willie Williams, who was in Philadelphia, said no prime suspect had been identified. The official spokesmen haughtily told everyone that the police were not re-sponsible for the continued leaks from within the department that were building pressure on O.J., burying him beneath a mountain of allegations that could not be traced. "Leaks are not a police issue," in-toned police spokesman Commander David Gascon. "Leaks are a media issue. . . . We just hope the media is responsible and noth-ing is done to damage the investigation." Meanwhile, the leaks underlined that police were now looking at Simpson not as a possi-ble suspect but as their *only* suspect. As in the Sherlock Holmes stories, the game was afoot.

In reality, the leaks from the police de-partment were threatening to become a flood. KCBS-TV reported that bits of flesh that could have been Simpson's had been found at the death scene. KCOP-TV reported that a bloody ski mask had been discovered in Simpson's home, and that Nicole's throat had been chopped with a military-style knife. The *Los Angeles Daily News* disputed that report, saying the murder weapon may have been a razor-sharp folding shovel of the type used by soldiers. The *Los Angeles Times* said a woman jogging on South Bundy the night of the slayings saw a vehicle matching the description of O.J. Simpson's white Bronco parked across the street from Nicole's town house. Everyone was quoting police sources as saying that O.J. was ripe for arrest within days. True or not, such public revelations were like big bells bonging in the heads of Robert Shapiro and O.J. Simpson and showed that the police department was a sieve of loose information. Somebody was having a field day sending messages through the media to play mind games with the suspect.

The strategy of the police department brass and the district attorney remained to proceed slowly, dot every "i," cross every "t." If and when they went after O.J., they wanted a clean grab made with enough evidence that they would not have to take a backward step. This time they would take no chances. The last thing they wanted was to be crucified again for being clumsy, so O.J. was accorded special treatment and a loose rein because he was a celebrity.

Meanwhile, O.J. was still free. Not out on bail, just out. He had not been charged, but the lawmen of Los Angeles felt that such a famous face, under such intense and constant scrutiny, was locked up about as tightly as possible under the circumstances. *USA Today* quoted a prominent defense lawyer, Harlan Braun, as saying, "O.J. can't run anywhere. Police are more worried about making a bad mistake."

Shapiro decided to counter the police findings with some independent efforts of his own, and inquiries went out around the nation seeking the help of top-level private investigators and forensic specialists. Shapiro wanted his own, independent tests, and had suggested that a second autopsy be done by his own experts on Nicole. Henry Lee, the director of the Forensic Science Laboratory in Connecticut and a specialist in reconstructing crime scenes, flew in from Hartford. Shapiro was soon joined by Michael Baden, the former chief pathologist for New York City and now a forensic scientist for the New York State Police. Shapiro had snared a couple of recognized professionals. Lee literally wrote the highly regarded book, *Introduction to Forensics*, and had been part of the successful defense team in the William Kennedy Smith rape trial. Baden was a consultant to the Warren Commission during the investigation of President Kennedy's assassination. Here was a preview of the kind of defense that could be mounted by someone with a lot of money. An indigent defendant would never have had such people on call. "We are focusing on doing as thorough an investigation as is humanly possible with the best experts in the world," lawyer Shapiro said.

The final DNA tests, radioactive probes of the blood samples which might provide an almost infallible genetic fingerprint that could place O.J. at the scene, were not expected to be completed for a number of weeks, and Shapiro needed to move much faster than that. But even with the experts, he would have a rough go, because the police were adamantly not tipping their hand. Since no one had yet been arrested in the crime, no lawyers or specialists were entitled to look at any evidence that the police had gathered. The cops were not even talking to the victims' families, and they sure were not going to spill the invaluable information to the prime suspect's lawyer. Shapiro said he wanted to offer his experts to the police to "help" in the investigation. Fat chance, replied the cops, not about to let any outsiders close to whatever they had found.

There were also indications that Shapiro was attempting to put together a talented team of lawyers to handle the courtroom side of the trial, if there was one, for at the moment, O.J. Simpson was still a free man. Already there was serious legal maneuvering underway, as the prosecution began talking about taking the case quickly to a Grand Jury for an indictment. That would allow them to avoid a swift preliminary hearing in which evidence would have to be exposed. Grand Jury sessions are so private that defense attorneys and even the defendant are not entitled to learn what goes on behind those closed doors.

There was a related, more pragmatic point in play, one that no one was willing to discuss. Since the Grand Jury would then be required to determine whether the death penalty should be sought, District Attorney Gil Garcetti could dodge that possible controversy in his upcoming race for reelection. That was another reason for the delay in arresting Simpson. The government wanted to be able to present a Grand Jury with evidence that the crime had been premeditated, which would help justify asking for the death penalty, and the evidence to make that leap had not yet been finalized. Two years earlier, Garcetti had won his job by criticizing the incumbent D.A., Ira Reiner. Now Garcetti, also a Brentwood resident, was at risk of being thrown in the cart and trundled to the same electoral guillotine. His assistants, Marcia Clark and David Conn, were working very, very closely with the police, but still no charges were being brought.

Special treatment for the superstar celebrity? Heaven forbid. Police Chief Williams was stung at the mere suggestion. "I'm satisfied that the investigation is moving appropriately. . . . We want to be careful," he said. "This is not taking a long time. It's been four business days. We're doing a very expeditious investigation while leaving no stone unturned.

"We are not doing anything special or extra because of Mr. Simpson. Most homicides are not solved in the first twenty-four hours—but you don't have people watching those cases."

Most of the street cops did not agree.They knew that if a homicide isn't solved within the first twenty-four hours, it tends to get more and more difficult.

Williams wasn't the only one concerned about the image tarnishing that seemed to be going on through the saturation coverage of the media. It was causing some problems for one specific corporation. Hertz was beginning to hurt. Joseph M. Russo, vice president for government and public affairs for the Hertz Corporation, wrote an indignant letter from the Park Ridge, New Jersey, headquarters to *USA Today* to challenge a statement made by the newspaper and the vice president of public affairs for PepsiCo. "Hertz has not attempted to dissociate [stet] itself from O.J. Simpson," Russo thundered.

He said Hertz had been working with O.J. for nineteen years and he had starred in "classic commercials, dashing through airport terminals to a chorus of 'Go, O.J., go!'" Simpson had run for football teams and "now he was running for us."

Taking the high and moral road, Russo deplored the "media feeding frenzy" and "ghoulish speculation" and said the proper stance was to "wait for the inevitable events to unfold" in a proper police investigation. Then he denied that Hertz had pulled some of the famed O.J. advertising spots. The truth, he said, was that the company had been using a new marketing strategy and O.J. "is not, in fact, featured in any of our recent advertising."

Russo wrote that Nicole and O.J. were both friends of the corporation and the personnel of the rental-car agency were "shocked and saddened." In conclusion, he mockingly thanked the newspaper and the PepsiCo official for their "advice," then dismissed them with a wave of the corporate hand. "You didn't know Nicole and O.J. Simpson," sniffed Russo. "We did and do."

Well, now. That ought to take care of that!

Chicago had not been forgotten in the police investigation. O.J. had flown there and spent a few hours before coming back, and the police had already found a bloody towel in his room that had been explained away by the cut hand. But was there more? Simpson had flown to Chicago with his golf clubs. Could something else, something that might have been a murder weapon, have been hidden in the big golf bag?

Two L.A. detectives had been flown to Chicago to liaise with the locals, and their efforts focused not on the hotel suite where Simpson had stayed but on a nearby vacant field that might have been the depository for a weapon or other potential evidence. Following an anonymous tip that a man resembling O.J. had been seen in the lot Monday morning, they scoured the field with pancake-shaped metal detectors, hunting the weapon that killed Nicole Simpson and Ron Goldman on the other side of the North American continent.

Perhaps the biggest break of the day came not from the investigating cops nor the unnamed leaks, but from a television tabloid show. *Hard Copy* had taken a copy of Shapiro's statement that O.J. was at home, waiting for the limo to the airport, and had done some elementary sleuthing that everyone else seemed to have bypassed. Their discovery was shocking. The driver of the limo who was dispatched to make that run said O.J. wasn't there when the car arrived at the estate at 10:45 P.M. In fact, the driver said, he showed up 15 minutes late and looked both agitated and sweaty.

It was classic proof of the basic idea in a criminal defense case—don't say anything to anybody, particularly to the police or a television camera. By offering O.J.'s explanation of awaiting the limo, Shapiro had locked them both into a bad spot. The *Hard Copy* disclosure made them look like liars.

Since the report had been viewed by a couple of dozen million people, it had to send the defense camp into a spin. O.J. still remained at large, and not charged with a crime. But things were looking bleak.

There was a final development in the day's events, one that would have extraordinary importance later. After the funeral, when the white limo in which Simpson had been riding returned to the mansion, the usual cozy game of hide-and-seek was temporarily abandoned. Cameras quickly zoomed in as he ran from the automobile to the front door, bent down, legs pumping just like he was back on the football field. Two bodyguards clung to him like big leeches, covering his head and face. This was most peculiar behavior, since the Juice's protectors had gone out of their way to keep the media from seeing him for the past several days, not infrequently yelling at cameramen and reporters to stay the hell away. Now they were making certain everyone had a peek.

The press immediately began to smell a rat and carefully studied the brief films of the hustling man in the black suit and the peculiar actions of his bodyguards. Two things popped up.

One of the bodyguards, a man on the Simpson security team payroll, was none other than a detective from the Los Angeles Police Department, moonlighting on the job with a double-murder suspect.

More important, the press concluded that the man who was running bent over and covered up was not O.J. at all, but Al Cowlings! In the blink of an eye, O.J. was gone. He had been at the funeral, in full view of hundreds, then—blip!—he was gone. The press corps felt like thousands of potential tacklers before them who had tried to snare the Juice.

Shapiro complained that a news helicopter had trailed his car, hoping it would lead him to where O.J. was now in seclusion. He would later say a press release had announced that Simpson was being moved out of the media way, but there was no such release, according to his own office.

And when Shapiro had come onto the case, he had promised the police full and complete cooperation. But now, he did not advise them of the exact address of where his client—the celebrity prime suspect in one of the most widely controversial double murders in American history—was staying. It was a gentleman's agreement. The lawyer was a gentleman. O.J. was a gentlemen. The cops and prosecution lawyers running the case were all ladies and gentlemen.

The routine would be that Simpson would be allowed privacy, on the condition that Shapiro would deliver him for surrender, if necessary, through a simple telephone call. Fine, everyone agreed. It's the sort of thing that is done every day, common currency in the land of law enforcement.

Within 24 hours, they would all look like a bunch of bumbling jerks.

14
FRIDAY,
JUNE 17

Felony Complaint for Arrest Warrant
Case No. BA097211

The undersigned is informed and believes that:

COUNT ONE

On or about June 12, 1994, in the county of Los Angeles, the crime of murder, in violation of Penal Code Section 187 (a), a Felony, was committed by Orenthal James Simpson, who did willfully, unlawfully, and with malice aforethought murder Nicole Brown Simpson, a human being.

Notice: The above offense is a serious felony within the meaning of Penal Code Section 1192.7 (c) (1).

It is further alleged that in the commission and attempted commission of the above offense, the said defendant(s), Orenthal James Simpson, personally used a deadly and dangerous weapon(s), to wit, knife, said use not being an element of the above offense, within the meaning of Penal Code Section 12022 (b) and also causing the above offense to be a serious felony within the meaning of Penal Code Section 1192.7 (c) (23).

COUNT TWO

On or about June 12, 1994, in the county of Los Angeles, the crime of murder, in violation of Penal Code Section 187 (a), a Felony, was committed by Orenthal James Simpson, who did willfully, unlawfully, and with malice aforethought murder Ronald Lyle Goldman, a human being.

Notice: The above offense is a serious felony within the meaning of Penal Code Section 1192.7 (c) (1).

It is further alleged that in the commission and attempted commission of the above offense, the said defendant(s), Orenthal James Simpson, personally used a deadly and dangerous weapon(s), to wit, knife, said use not being an element of the above offense, within the meaning of Penal Code Section 12022 (b) and also causing the above offense to be a serious felony within the meaning of Penal Code Section 1192.7 (c) (23).

It is further alleged as to Counts 1 and 2 the defendant has in this proceeding been convicted of more than one offense of murder in the first or second degree within the meaning of Penal Code Section 190.2 (a) (3).

Further, attached hereto and incorporated herein are official reports and documents of a law enforcement agency which the undersigned believes establishes probable cause for the arrest of defendant(s), Orenthal James Simpson, for the above-listed crimes. Wherefore, a warrant of arrest is requested for Orenthal James Simpson.

I declare under penalty of perjury that the foregoing is true and correct and that this complaint, Case Number BA097211, consists of 2 count(s).

Executed at Los Angeles, County of Los Angeles, on June 17, 1994.

Phillip Vannatter
(LAPD Robbery-Homicide detective)
Declarant and Complainant

The felony complaint was filed by District Attorney Gil Garcetti against O.J. Simpson early Friday morning. Under California law, such a document is required to establish probable cause for an arrest. O.J. was formally charged and the game was over. Or was it?

At this vital point, the house of cards built by the gentlemen representing the prosecution and defense teams collapsed. They had taken it on faith that O.J. Simpson, a man whose entire lifetime had been spent getting out of jams, would sit still and do nothing when the time came to take him into custody. As Peter Arenelly, a law professor at UCLA, observed in a television interview, "His face is known across the world. Mr. Simpson is not going to flee. Given that there is no risk of flight in this case, arrest doesn't need to be done immediately."

At 8:30 A.M., police telephoned Robert Shapiro, O.J.'s lawyer, and told him that the formal complaints had been filed and that he must surrender his client. Since the cops had no idea where O.J. had been since leaving his house at 360 Rockingham Avenue the day of Nicole's funeral—apparently sympathetic that such a celebrity couldn't put up with the media circus outside his home—Shapiro was their contact. The police chose not to send a black-and-white squad car with a couple of burly cops around and haul the dude away. Relaying the message through the lawyer bought O.J. more time.

An hour later, Shapiro drove to the secluded San Fernando Valley hillside home of Simpson's friend Robert Kardashian and broke the news to O.J. that surrender time would be 11 A.M. Simpson had been heavily sedated for several days and under the care of a doctor, and was just struggling up from a drug-induced sleep when his lawyer arrived.

More time passed, with Shapiro, who was legally an officer of the court, calling police every 15 minutes with an update. A doctor was summoned to examine a swollen lymph node in one of O.J.'s armpits. O.J. asked for some time alone, then updated his will through a telephone call to his lawyer. This might have raised an eyebrow or two, since people who potentially face long jail terms are not usually concerned about the proper disposal of their property when they die. But on this occasion it did not, probably because no one in the house filling with friends and professionals on the growing defense team, including four doctors, thought that O.J., one of the greatest runners ever to play the game of football, might rabbit.

The clocks ticked inexorably on, and soon it was 11 A.M., the appointed time for O.J. to be given over to the police. The designated hour passed and the minutes ticked away, until at 11:45 A.M. the police began to realize things were not going quite as well as anticipated. The complaint had been issued several hours earlier, and now, the cops told Shapiro, they considered O.J. to be a fugitive from justice. He would be arrested on sight. While O.J. was wailing in a downstairs room, Shapiro spoke over the noise, giving the police the address of the house and a patrol car was finally dispatched. The lawyer did not tell O.J. the police were on their way.

That a terrible mistake had been made became apparent in a blinding flash of realization.

O.J. had not been alone at that critical time, for the house contained a number of people. But he *was* in a room that was separated from the others, and for company he had only one person—his most trusted friend, Al Cowlings, who had always been ready to walk through a wall of fire for the Juice.

When they went to collect O.J., the room

was empty. O.J. had decided to run for daylight one last time.

From 11 A.M. until 1:50 P.M., there was a lot of teeth-gnashing by men and women in dress-for-success suits and blue uniforms with shiny badges. Instead of "To Protect and Serve" the police motto for the day could have been "Oh my God, No!" Absolutely the worst thing in the world had just happened. Forget the earthquake. Forget the riots. The Juice was loose! A tidal wave of horrible publicity was headed straight for the Parker Center Police Headquarters and it was time to duck and cover.

The lead article in *Time* magazine's next issue put it succinctly. "When asked how they could have let the most famous double-murder suspect in history slip away under their noses, the angry police commander and the tight-faced lawyer and the whole choir of commentators all said the same thing, without a trace of irony: 'We never thought he would run.'"

They were as wrong as wrong could be. The Juice was loose.

LAPD Police Commander David J. Gascon had the unenviable job of stepping before the assembled media to make a statement. All morning, the news of the complaint had been known and the television circus had shifted to the police headquarters, where Simpson was due to arrive. But hours dragged by and O.J. didn't show. Reporters began telling a growing television audience that something wasn't right, although there was no information on what the problem might be. Gascon, a trim officer with a casual and distinct manner, who usually appeared in a civilian suit to soften the cop image, had been the official spokesman for the entire Simpson affair, always guarded in his comments, but rather relaxed amid the frenzy of news conferences. But when he approached the bouquet of microphones on Friday, he was in full blue regalia, shield and collar stars polished and a row of honor ribbons across his chest. He stood at military attention, jaw clenched, almost quivering in rage. Police Chief Williams was in Philadelphia, far from the fray, and Gascon was served up instead.

"Mr. Simpson, in an agreement with his attorney, was scheduled to surrender this morning to the Los Angeles Police Department. Initially, that was 11 o'clock. Then it became 11:45. Mr. Simpson has not appeared. The Los Angeles Police Department is also very unhappy with the activities surrounding his failure to surrender. We will continue our pursuit of Mr. Simpson and hope to have him in custody soon."

The tidal wave hit. There was a moment of astonished silence from the newspeople, then they erupted with questions, which Gascon parried, pointing out the cautious manner in which the case had been handled. But he flared if any reporter hinted that there might have been just a little bitsy, teensy-weensy fault in the way the cops handled the case.

"Our official comments have been limited to those statements given at the crime scene by Lieutenant John Rogers . . . comments by Chief Williams and comments that I've made," he bristled. "Any criticism of the Los Angeles Police Department because of what has been published or broadcast by the media is unfair. We do not control your newsrooms." That was a nice answer, but nobody had asked such a question. Since the media didn't have the taxpayer-sponsored job of arresting people, they wanted to know why O.J. wasn't sitting in a jail cell. Gascon denied that any preferential treatment had been given to O.J. It was a good performance by a spokesman who was drowning on stage before a television audience that by now stretched across the nation. When he mentioned that the police had done a magnificent job, he appeared to flush in embarrassment as reporters and photographers laughed.

Gascon did, however, promise that O.J. Simpson would be caught—again—and brought in. "We will find him." It would not be easy, for at that moment, the cops didn't have a clue where O.J. might be.

Even as he spoke, a statewide bulletin chattered over the teletypes of the California Highway Patrol and relayed to other law enforcement agencies. Police already had sent officers to watch the flights at LAX and notified the Border Patrol at crossing points to Mexico. In doing the magnificent job, described by Gascon, police had not confiscated the passport of a man who had enough money to go anywhere in the world.

Now it was Gil Garcetti's turn before the microphones, and the Los Angeles County District Attorney, stormed into the news conference in the Downtown Criminal Courts Building looking like he was about to blow a gasket. Trim, every gray hair in place, immaculately dressed and madder than hell, the D.A. apparently had decided that the best defense was a good offence.

"Now you can tell that I'm a little upset and I *am* upset. This is a very serious case.

Many of us, perhaps, had empathy to some extent. We saw, perhaps, the falling of an American hero. To some extent, I viewed Mr. Simpson in the same way. But let's remember we have two innocent people who have been brutally killed. We have their families who are still with us today who are going to suffer for the rest of their lives, including the children of the Simpsons."

This should have been one of Garcetti's grandest moments. He should have been able to announce the arrest of O.J. Simpson and bask in the glory of a job well done on a high-profile case. It is difficult to appear as a hero when you have to stand before a nationwide television audience with egg dripping from your nose. But he had to get things back on track and he did, in a hurry, by issuing a stern warning to the public. "If you in any way are assisting Mr. Simpson in avoiding justice . . . you are committing a felony. . . . I'll guarantee you that if there is any evidence that you assisted Mr. Simpson . . . you will be prosecuted as a felon."

He carefully danced around pointing a finger of blame, other than saying, after all, the media had surrounded Simpson's house and "let him get away." It was a cheap shot, because the press carried only cameras and notebooks, not badges, and had not agreed to allow O.J. to hide out at some unknown address.

Immediately, there was wide speculation on where the Juice might be. Some were convinced he was already out of the country. Others envisioned O.J. frantically trying to prove his innocence while on the run, not unlike the popular motion picture *The Fugitive*. But still others considered that O.J. had nowhere to run, nowhere to hide, and probably was suicidal.

Television audiences were growing to extraordinary numbers, Super Bowl kind of ratings, as friends told friends about the news conferences explaining why O.J. Simpson was out there somewhere, running.

Shapiro also had some heavy explaining to do, so he, too, met with the press. After all, it was his client who had flown the coop while the lawyer was standing in the very same house. He was a man who thought he had seen just about everything the law had to offer in the way of stormy and controversial cases, from the early days when he defended porn queen Linda Lovelace to the recent negotiations he had made that brought Erik Menendez back from Israel. Never something like this. All he could do, like Gascon and Garcetti before him, was to bite the bullet of reality and get on with things. "I've never felt worse in my professional career," he said. "I've always kept my word and my clients have always kept their word."

He described O.J. as having been emotionally frail and fragile, and for the first time mentioned that he considered Simpson potentially suicidal.

"We were never concerned he might run," the lawyer told the press. "I believe having four physicians there and his best friend—a former football player—there's no way we could have been better prepared."

Shapiro, a news conference veteran, quickly got past the explanation, sounding almost convincing in his argument that nobody was to blame for what had happened. He knew the press feeds on new material, so he rolled them a bomb.

O.J., he said, had written three letters before he left the building; one to his children, one to his mother, and one for the public. Then he stepped aside, allowing Robert Kardashian to step to the microphones. He was another of O.J.'s oldest friends, had known him since the USC days, and as a lawyer had been helping advise Simpson during his time of trouble. He unfolded a letter that had been printed on white paper in black ink, with some words scratched out, others added. In a somber voice, to a hushed audience, he began to read the letter O.J. had written to his public.

To whom it may concern:

First, everyone understand I have nothing to do with Nicole's murder. I loved her. I always have and I always will. If we had a problem, it's because I loved her so much.

Recently we came to the understanding that for now we were not right for each other, at least for now. Despite our love, we were different and that's why we mutually agreed to go our separate ways.

It was tough splitting up for a second time, but we both knew it was for the best. Inside, I had no doubt that in the future we would be close friends or more. Unlike what has been written in the press, Nicole and I had a great relationship for most of our lives together. Like all long-term relationships, we had a few downs and ups.

I took the heat New Year's 1989 because that's what I was supposed to do. I did not plead no contest for any other reason but to protect our privacy, and was advised it would end the press hype.

I don't want to belabor knocking the press but I can't believe what is being said. Most of it is totally made up. I know you have a job to do but as a last wish, please, please, please leave my children in peace. Their lives will be tough enough.

I want to send my love and thanks to all my friends. I'm sorry I can't name every one of you, especially A.C. Man, thanks for being in my life. The support and friendship I received from so many: Wayne Hughes, Lewis Markes, Frank Olson, Mark Packer, Bender, Bobby Kardashian. I wish we had spent more time together in recent years. My golfing buddies, Hoss, Alan Austin, Mike, Craig, Bender, Wyler, Sandy, Jay, Donnie, thanks for all the fun.

All my teammates over the years, Reggie, you were the soul of my pro career. Ahmad, I never stopped being proud of you. Marcus; you've got a great lady in Catherine, don't mess it up. Bobby Chandler, thanks for always being there. Skip and Cathy, I love you guys, without you I never would have made it through this far.

Marguerite, thanks for the early years. We had some fun. Paula, what can I say? You are special. I'm sorry I'm not going to have, we're not going to have our chance. God brought you to me, I now see. As I leave, you'll be in my thoughts.

I think of my life and feel I've done most

of the right things. So why do I end up like this? I can't go on. No matter what the outcome, people will look and point. I can't take that. I can't subject my children to that. This way they can move on and go on with their lives.

Please, if I've done anything worthwhile in my life, let my kids live in peace from you, the press.

I've had a good life. I'm proud of how I lived. My mama taught me to do unto others. I treated people the way I wanted to be treated. I've always tried to be up and helpful, so why is this happening? I'm sorry for the Goldman family. I know how much it hurts.

Nicole and I had a good life together. All this press talk about a rocky relationship was no more than what every long-term relationship experiences. All her friends will confirm that I have been totally loving and understanding of what she's been going through.

At times I have felt like a battered husband or boyfriend but I loved her, make that clear to everyone. And I would take whatever it took to make it work.

Don't feel sorry for me. I've had a great life, great friends. Please think of the real O.J. and not this lost person.

Thanks for making my life special. I hope I helped yours.

Peace and love,

O.J.

In the "O" of his name, Simpson had jotted a pair of eyes, a nose and an upswept mouth—a happy face.

Shapiro answered an obvious question with an obvious answer. He said that in his opinion and that of four doctors, what the startled reporters and the public had just heard was a suicide note.

15
O.J.'s Last Run

"He is a wanted murder suspect and we will go find him," LAPD's Gascon had pledged. They did, but not without a bit of luck.

After they had been missing all afternoon, Cowlings and Simpson were spotted at 5:25 P.M. by a young couple heading out for a weekend camping trip. The two men were in a white Ford Bronco, Cowlings at the wheel and O.J. in the backseat. The motorists said they had a clear view of Simpson and he stared back at them "like he was death." They gave a quick, excited call to the police. Combined with some monitoring the police had been doing of the frequency of Cowlings' cellular telephone, they were able to alert units in the area.

Orange County Deputy Sheriff Larry Pool, patroling the busy Interstate 5 Freeway near the exit for the El Toro Marine base, spotted the Bronco, goosed his patrol car up close, and read the license plate. It matched the one that every law enforcement officer in California had been seeking. As Pool dropped back to a careful distance behind the white truck, other police cars sped to the area, closing off exits and falling into a pack. Soon, police cars were trailing the Bronco in lines three deep and spread across every lane of the wide freeway, lights flashing, letting nothing pass.

Up in the sky, a covey of police and news helicopters swarmed to the scene, risking a midair collision to follow the action.

One of the most famous people in America was on the run, his entire lifetime of celebrity trashed by his earlier escape. The police had him in their sights now, and he would not get away again.

Then the TV cameras in the choppers focused on the caravan stretching out along the freeway and stations across America began tuning in the transmissions to relay the pictures to the audience. What would become one of the most dramatic television events of the decade was unfolding, as the

Bronco rolled along, trailed by a five-lane-wide tail of twenty police cars.

O.J. Simpson, one of the most famous murder suspects in American history, had vanished, was feared to have committed suicide during the long hours without contact, and now was riding along Interstate 5, with a gun to his head. It did not take a rocket scientist to figure out why news directors at television stations around the country ordered the broadcasts to be carried live.

Al Cowlings flipped on his flashing hazard lights and wove carefully through traffic, staying well below the speed limit, almost like a driver who knew a cop was following and did not want to get stopped for a traffic violation. But he knew that much more was at stake and wanted the police to understand what was happening inside the Bronco. At 6:46 P.M., he picked up his cellular telephone and, using his thumb, punched the emergency 911 number.

OFFICER: 911. What are you reporting?

COWLINGS: This is A.C. I have O.J. in the car.

OFFICER: O.K., where are you?

COWLINGS: Please, I'm coming up the Five freeway.

OFFICER: O.K.

COWLINGS: Right now we all, we're O.K., but you got to tell the police just to back off. He's still alive. He's got a gun to his head.

OFFICER: O.K. Hold on a minute . . . Monica.

COWLINGS: He just wants to see his mother. Let me get him to the house.

OFFICER: Hold on a moment, O.K. Where are you? Is everything else O.K.?

COWLINGS: Everything right now is O.K., officer. Everything is O.K. He wants me to get him to his mom. He wants me to get him to his house.

OFFICER: O.K.

COWLINGS: All I . . . That's all we ask. He's got a gun to his head.

OFFICER: O.K., and sir, what's your name?

COWLINGS: My name is A.C. You know who I am, Goddam it.

OFFICER: O.K. All-righty, sir, hold on just a moment.

OFFICER TWO: Hi. What's your name?

COWLINGS: Aww . . . (Hangs up)

Eventually, Detective Fred Lange, one of the lead investigators on the case, managed to establish contact with Cowlings on the portable telephone. He had talked to both men previously, and they knew who he was. Lange stayed calm as Cowlings told him

207

that a distraught O.J. was in the back of the Ford, pointing a pistol at his own chin. He told Lange that O.J. had vowed never to surrender. But he did want to see his mother.

Go easy, Lange advised, actually talking with O.J. Don't hurt yourself or anyone else. We can work something out. Occasionally, as Lange tried to bring Simpson to a halt, O.J. would abruptly hang up the telephone. Lange would call back. He was told that if O.J. didn't get what he wanted, that he would pull the trigger. With the nature of the morose letter well-known by this time, and the assumption that he had been on his way to Nicole's grave when the car was spotted, suicide was still a strong possibility.

Slowly the strange caravan, in the full eye of television, headed north on the Five, then turned west on the 91 briefly, then north again on the 405, like a giant mouse running through the maze of Los Angeles' web of interstate highways. Startled motorists in front of the macabre parade were shocked to look in their rear-view mirrors and find O.J. Simpson and an army of police hot on their tails. They quickly pulled aside as Cowlings deftly steered around them.

Unknown to O.J., it was almost impossible for the cops to contact his mother. The pressure of the situation had overcome Eunice Simpson, who had flown home after Nicole's funeral. She had been rushed to the California Pacific Medical Center in San Francisco for undisclosed reasons.

As the television cameras recorded every move, radio stations got into the act, broadcasting simultaneously in hopes the fugitives were listening to their car radio. Carrying live broadcast reports, the talk-show hosts got an earful of supporters—people O.J. had never met—calling on him to surrender, to do himself no harm. Friends, too, called in. "Please, think of your children," pleaded another football great, Walter Payton, the retired running star of the Chicago Bears. Vince Evans, quarterback of the Los Angeles Raiders, broke down and wept, "Please stop. In Jesus' name, just stop. We love you, man." Shapiro had sounded the call first, at the news conference, saying, "O.J., wherever you are, for the sake of your family, for the sake of your children, please surrender immediately." Now all of America was sending the same thought to Simpson as he rode, overcome with grief and confusion, in the back seat of Cowlings' Bronco. He was a man en route to destiny.

On the evening that Los Angeles stood

still, as if a heart seized in terror had briefly stopped, CBS, CNN, and ABC went to full live coverage of the unfolding tragedy, and NBC interrupted a National Basketball Association championship game to try and broadcast both things at the same time. The surreal image from above the white Bronco on the road, followed by so many police cars, was like watching a real-life drama in slow motion. In one astonishing development, sports broadcaster Al Michaels was giving a play-by-play on the situation, almost as if he were telling the audience about another marvelous run by O.J. Simpson. Indeed, the sports network ESPN was also carrying the live drama. Some people couldn't watch television, such as the cops in Buffalo, New York, who huddled around a radio in the police station, as the man who put the Bills on the football map played out his hand in California. Everywhere across the nation—in bars, health clubs, stores, and private homes—people gathered in front of television sets and around radios obsessed with the tragedy.

The bizarre realization would break into a viewer's consciousness periodically that this wasn't some popular, made-for-TV movie with a fabled outlaw playing a depersonalized game of cops and robbers. The

man in the back of the white vehicle thread-
ing through traffic was accused of murder-
ing his ex-wife and one of her friends. Simpson was wanted for brutally killing two
people, but in this dramatic moment, he
was reclaiming his hero status, whether he
wanted it or not.

As the radio and television broadcasts
penetrated the Los Angeles area, huge
crowds began to gather on highway over-
passes and motorists who found themselves
on either side of the same freeway pulled to
the side and got out of their cars. People
left businesses and scrambled up highway
embankments. The Bronco and its accompa-
nying police cars drove between walls of
human flesh. Among the millions of people
watching television that evening were a pair
of Los Angeles cops, trained hostage negoti-
ators, who were hoping for the opportunity
to talk with O.J. Simpson.

As the Bronco whizzed past the lines of
fans, they waved, honked horns, pointed and
yelled encouragement to O.J. There was not
a chance that he would escape, nor any
reason for them to be cheering a murder
suspect, but that wasn't some mere mortal
in the back seat of the Bronco. "Go! Go! Go!"
some cried, pumping their fists, desperate to

show support, as if O.J. was five yards away from paydirt and hell-bent for the goal line.

After some speculation that he might be heading for the airport to try and catch a plane out of the country, the Ford Bronco drove past LAX, finally leaving the freeway at Sunset Boulevard. Cowlings slowed to move through a thick swarm of people who were almost delirious in their screams, some of them lunging into the street to touch the car as if to put a fingerprint on history. By this time, police realized Simpson was headed back home, and they scrambled a 25-man Special Weapons and Tactics team to the mansion. When the heavily armed SWAT unit arrived, dozens of people were already shoving into the street outside and some were trying to scale the ivy-covered walls, being thrown back by police like fish from a pond. An unreasoning mania had gripped the crowd, which was growing by the minute.

Fifteen minutes after the SWAT team got there, the white Bronco turned into the street. Police cordoned off the crowd and opened the gate so the car could pull into the cobblestone driveway without stopping. When it did, a police cruiser plugged the gap behind it and the other following police cars stuffed into the street, bumper to bumper, wheel to wheel.

Out of nowhere, a young black man wearing jeans and a white T-shirt broke into a sprint, three cops at his heels. Jason Simpson flashed his father's agility, as he went up and over a police cruiser and through the gate, startling Al Cowlings, who had just come to a stop after a 60-mile odyssey that had left him exhausted and shaking. Jason grabbed the door handle and A.C. roughly pushed him away. He would not be allowed to talk to his dad, who was clutching a rosary, a pair of family photographs, and a blue-steel revolver. Two policemen stepped carefully from the house, took Jason by each arm and brought him inside.

The car was at a stop, but the crowd beyond the walls bubbled like a kettle. "Free O.J.," they yelled. "Save the Juice!" Not a word about the murdered Nicole. Not a word about dead young Ron Goldman. "We love the Juice!" A woman almost remembered Nicole, then discarded the thought, as if it were heresy. "He was a victim, too," she said.

"I just had to bring my family to see this," said one middle-aged man with a child on his shoulders, as youths nearby began to rock a police car back and forth. Another agreed. "It's like when we went to see Elvis at Graceland."

A lone helicopter clattered overhead and settled just above the trees, the eyes of its TV camera centered on the Bronco, feeding reports to one of the largest television audiences ever to watch anything. The pilot described seeing O.J. Simpson, sitting below with a pistol in his hand.

The next major problem for the cops was how to handle the increasingly volatile Al Cowlings. Dressed in black and pumped full of adrenaline, he was bordering on being out of control after enduring hours of stress. He was a man trapped in the middle of a nightmare with the life of his best friend at stake. A.C. would occasionally get out of the Bronco, reluctant to leave his buddy, even for a moment, to tell police, "Don't do anything stupid. Get the police away."

Other requests may have been possible on that balmy evening in the middle of June, but not that one. Already SWAT team members were in position, hiding in shrubbery near the Bronco or higher up, with huge sniper rifles pointed at O.J.'s head. O.J. Simpson would not be allowed to escape again, under any conditions.

Peter Weireter, a seventeen-year veteran of SWAT negotiations, was now in phone contact with O.J., talking smoothly, quietly to a confused and frightened man. Their biggest fear at this point was not O.J. escaping, or even of the former superstar taking his own life. There was only one way for the situation to deteriorate beyond police control now, and that would be if Simpson came out of the Bronco firing his pistol. It is known in the trade as "suicide by cop" and the men and women in blue feared it viscerally, as evening shadows grew long around the big house and spread over the driveway.

They also didn't want to arrest or handcuff Cowlings within sight of O.J., fearing that seeing his friend manhandled might push Simpson over the edge. O.J. still had a gun and had to be considered dangerous.

Other officers finally coaxed Cowlings into the house, out of O.J.'s sight and placed him under arrest. But when the batteries in O.J.'s phone died, they had to let A.C. go again, briefly, to deliver new ones to Simpson. After that, he was back in handcuffs, to be booked on suspicion of harboring a fugitive, with bail set at $250,000.

Shapiro arrived at the mansion and went inside, where Robert Kardashian was also awaiting the final act.

The Bronco, containing the most famous fugitive in the United States, sat in the driveway, its hazard lights monotonously blinking as the sun began to set and the television pictures that had transfixed America began to fade.

It had been a terrible episode to watch. It had been impossible to ignore. Everyone stayed tuned, hoping for the best, fearing the worst, or at least a good camera angle if he pulled the trigger.

Finally, using no force greater than a soft voice and an understanding nature honed by years of negotiations, Weireter brought the dramatic episode to a nonviolent end. At 8:50 P.M., in the dark, O.J. Simpson laid his wood-handled pistol on a green towel in the cargo area of the Bronco and climbed out, still clutching the rosary and the family pictures. Weireter alerted the SWAT snipers to hold their fire, that Simpson was no longer armed.

O.J. almost staggered up the short walkway between his driveway and his front door, and collapsed into the arms of waiting policemen. There is a strange bond called the "Stockholm Syndrome," in which captors and hostages bond together over a period of time. It clicked in here. Instead of slamming the murder suspect to the floor, putting a gun to his head and clamping on the handcuffs, police allowed O.J. to use the bathroom, talk to his hospitalized mother, and then handed him something to drink. Orange Juice. Simpson was as apologetic as a contrite child caught stealing cookies, apologizing repeatedly to the policemen and shaking their hands. "I'm sorry for putting you guys out," he told cops. "I'm sorry for making you do this." Then he turned to the waiting detectives and was arrested.

A short time later, wearing a dark blazer over a yellow polo shirt, he was loaded into a police car, sandwiched in back between two detectives, and taken by a special motorcade to Parker Center, where he was booked at 10 P.M. on two counts of murder. A mugshot showing a man who was utterly wilted by exhaustion and strain, was taken, numbered BK4013970 06-17-94.

O.J. Simpson, a man whose name will be remembered forever in the annals of sports, entertainment, and crime, was locked in a little 7-by-4-foot cell at L.A.'s Men's Central Jail. A deputy popped open the cell-door window every quarter-hour for a look to make sure the prisoner had not harmed himself.

O.J.'s last run, his longest and most famous, came to an end with him sitting alone in a tiny room, surrounded by steel walls and under lock and key. But even those

dismal surroundings were more spacious
and infinitely better than Nicole Brown
Simpson and Ronald Lyle Goldman had
that night.

Epilogue

Hertz caved in fast. In sharp contrast to the almost pugilistic letter written by the company's vice president the previous day, a news release was rushed out when the murder complaints were announced. "Hertz is shocked and saddened by this development," it said, and the long, mutually lucrative association between Hertz and its primary spokesperson came to a jarring halt. No more would we see O.J. hurtling airport benches or running to a waiting automobile, smiling and advising consumers, "Go nonstop to your car with your name in lights!" His name was now on the minds of most people in America. Like it or not, however, he was still associated with those Hertz advertisements, a joke surfacing that O.J.'s recent dash through LAX and O'Hare gave new meaning to his running through airports.

NBC executives then had to huddle quickly. O.J. was halfway through his television sports contract and had completed a TV pilot called *Frogmen*. *Playboy* had to rethink the release of a newly completed Simpson exercise video for men.

Hertz was only the latest company to find itself steam-rollered by a celebrity spokesperson who tripped over his or her image, dragging the corporate logo down with them. Most such corporations, when they were stung, unceremoniously dumped the superstar. Pepsi lopped off Michael Jackson when the globally popular singer became embroiled in a sexual molestation charge with a young boy. The ever-dangerous Madonna also was given her walking papers by Pepsi after performing the musical video *Like A Prayer*, which was considered by many to be sacrilegious.

Actor Burt Reynolds lost a lucrative gig with the Florida orange growers when wife Loni Anderson filed for divorce, and tennis player Jennifer Capriati had just developed her All-American sweetness when she was buried commercially because of a drug possession rap. Olympic skater Nancy Kerrigan found herself on thin ice with Disney shortly after winning the silver medal for allegedly bad-mouthing Mickey Mouse. Heroes and heroines all, and now O.J. Simpson's name was flashing among those dim stars. The only thing that was increasing in value for him were his sports trading cards and items he had autographed, since the savvy investing ten-year-olds were suddenly betting that Simpson might not be around to sign too many more autographs. Rarity is king in the card market, where Simpson's rookie NFL card had been valued at $125 and suddenly rose in both demand and price. Hero-shmero, kids play for keeps.

The advertisements were only one form of media attention being paid to O.J., and by Friday morning it was all negative. Since Monday, the press that had once lionized him had begun to batter him endlessly. He had faithfully courted them over the years, unfailingly polite, ever ready to answer questions, always the gentleman. Now he was the latest sacrificial lamb to television Nielsen ratings and newspaper circulation numbers. Those charged with gathering information camped out at the O.J. estate around the clock, as their bosses weighed the public interest against personal privacy. Public interest won easily.

This was not new either, and O.J. was just the latest in a line of recent people declared semi-guilty by the voracious media, even before they stepped into court. The legal system that insisted everyone was innocent until proven guilty lay in tatters before the thundering media herd. Superstars like Michael Jackson and Woody Allen, midlevel names like Tonya Harding, and nobodies such as John and Lorena Bobbitt, Amy Fisher and Joey Buttafuocco were perhaps among the handful of people who could really feel sympathy for O.J. Simpson on Friday morning.

The huge interest came because O.J. had spent a lifetime crossing lines. He not only was a sports star, he also was an entertainment figure in Tinseltown, where a minor scandal is cause for hoopla and a major one is never far away. After all, O.J. lived in the same glossy neighborhood where sexy screen queen Marilyn Monroe committed suicide. His Brentwood neighbors included Los Angeles Mayor Richard Riordan, District Attorney Garcetti, and fellow movie stars Angela Lansbury, Meg Ryan and Dennis Quaid, Roseanne Arnold, Tom Hanks, Michelle Pfeiffer, and Meryl Streep.

Other Hollywood scandals included old-time megastar Fatty Arbuckle, who endured a rape and manslaughter trial in 1920 that ruined him, even though he was found innocent after three trials. Lana Turner's daughter, Cheryl, stabbed her mother's gangster boyfriend, Johnny Stompanato. Director Roman Polanski lost his actress wife Sharon Tate to Charlie Manson's mob of murderers, then had to flee the country himself to avoid a charge of having sex with a 13-year-old girl. Drugs, punchouts, divorces, and million-dollar contracts are everyday events. Hooray for Hollywood.

But those people were *just* movie stars. O.J. was a sports legend too, an icon, a role model, a nice guy. Even in disgrace, he was getting more coverage than any ordinary actor could have imagined. It seemed like a movie-of-the-week that couldn't find an ending.

In days gone by, when newspapers ruled the roost, a news event drew only a handful of reporters. Even at the White House, the press corps could fit comfortably in the Oval Office and chat with the President.

Television changed all that. Video took the lead in the news business. Stations were required to do some local programming, not just run brain-rot situation comedies, and it came as a pleasant surprise when station and network owners found that news could make a good buck for them from advertisers. The management discovered that investing in top-notch equipment, exotic satellite gear, even renting expensive helicopters, was better than putting the money in an interest-bearing bank account. Nothing could match the image of a breathless report popping up on the screen on the evening news, reported *live* from the scene of some cataclysmic event.

It was even better if the reporter were a local personality that might be seen riding around on normal days in a strange truck loaded down with cables and satellite gear, the station logo emblazoned on its side. So for covering celebrity stories like Tonya and Michael and O.J., it was no longer enough to let tony correspondents from the big networks handle the job. An elderly anchorman on Denver's KCNC Channel 4 accused an instant book on a hot topic of being sleaze, then immediately switched to the station's own correspondent who had flown to Oregon to cover disgraced ice skater Tonya Harding, whose big news that day was running barefoot across a parking lot trying to avoid reporters.

The flights into LAX throughout the week after the murders brought loads of young correspondents from the backwaters of American journalism, all of whom were out to earn their spurs by just covering the hell out of the O.J. story. Chatting back to the anchors at home on two-way video hookups, they almost bounced on their toes in efforts to appear calm. However, at the scene in Brentwood, they could do little more than stand around and hope it didn't get too hot before they had to go on the air. Sweat doesn't look good on camera. Since there were so many in the swarm, from all time zones, somebody was always standing before a camera, talking.

Then came the onslaught of the tabloid television shows, those take-no-prisoner, quick-draw video merchants whose egos seem to be in inverse proportion to talent. They have a reason to have big egos, for as America turned away from newspapers and toward television as its primary source of news, producers of sexy, exciting news nuggets not only could compete with the big networks, but they could excel! Couch potatoes across America loved them for opening their fat checkbooks to buy people to step in front of the camera and spill their secrets.

That does not mean that the big dogs

didn't also get into the scrap. Prestige was involved. The nets had people on the scene, and the ordinary journalistic folk had to make room for them, because, by God, you don't get in the way of a net! CNN was going live at the drop of a hat, and crews from foreign lands, where Hollywood goings on are always hot news, joined the throng. By midweek, they all started to get tired and tempers flared between rival cameramen trying to stick their lenses into a car window, any car window, and worry about who was inside later.

With television currently drenched with as many newsmagazine shows as it was once saturated in cowboy horse operas, even more producers, sound and camera crews, and correspondents showed up. Their stories would appear in the prime-time slots, slickly done but covering the same ground covered by everyone else. As the story grew in importance, it was not unusual for a viewer to see the latest O.J. developments on the local news, then watch it on the network evening news shows, catch a snappy version of events on a tabloid show, and then have a network special appear, followed by the late evening news and perhaps a talk-show roundtable about midnight. The cycle would begin anew the next morning, as soon as the Los Angeles newspapers hit the streets with the latest scoops from the "we're not saying anything" police department. Even the normally sedate *This Week with David Brinkley* show on Sunday morning postponed its discussion of North Korea's nuclear threat to debate the O.J. predicament.

Newspaper reporters, not as well-dressed or having as much hair, but less deranged, were not tied to the microphone cables that hobbled the TV types. Some played the stakeout game, but most preferred legwork, tracking sources and interviewing people far away from Hysteria Central. Every newspaper in the country was giving Simpson front-page play.

What made the situation truly weird was that the police were almost cooperative, intent on *using* the press reports to leak scary information to Simpson, his lawyers, and the District Attorney's office. They could roll out a bombshell and then sit back and watch what happened, all the while pretending that nobody was talking to any reporter. Despite the inevitable backlash of criticism, the reporters weren't just sitting around making up these allegations and tidbits. Someone in authority was willingly giving them out.

Audiences marveled at the audacity and lack of restraint shown by journalists, and the talk shows filled up quickly with media critics. Talker Rush Limbaugh intoned, "I don't think he did it," and his listeners, always in agreement, nodded knowingly. Either way, there was a rush to judgment.

It was a double-edged sword. The same people who protested the most gobbled up every word they could find on the tragedy of the fallen hero. Demographic studies run regularly by the media showed the audience was out there, and it was big and it was growing. It even included the present White House incumbent. President Clinton tactfully said that the situation involving "lost loved ones and a man widely admired in this country" was "a genuine tragedy."

From Sunset Boulevard to Pennsylvania Avenue, the moment-by-moment drama unfolding in Los Angeles captured an incredibly large audience. "It's the murder case everyone is talking about," said Jane Pauley on *Dateline NBC*.

But in their rush to gather every shred of news, to be *first* with some tidbit and rely so heavily on anonymous sources, the reporters did not take time to be careful. Instead of double-sourcing controversial reports, or reflecting on whether something was even logical, they hurled it onto the airwaves and into print immediately, and some of it was dreadfully wrong. One TV reporter speculated there was a suicide at the crime scene, and another claimed the murder weapon had been taken from the location where Simpson had been acting in a new film. And there had been no bloody ski mask found at the Simpson residence, as was reported by one person and repeated, parrot-like, by everyone else. All in all, it was a shoddy journalistic performance, with almost every media element reduced to the level of the tabloid gossipmongers.

Law enforcement agencies, likewise, failed to cover themselves in glory on this one. Trying to make up for their errors with a very good performance in the final hours, they were able to divert some attention from the horrible bobbles from earlier in the week. There was no question that O.J. Simpson was accorded star-quality treatment, and there was no question that the police and prosecutors paid a heavy price. After all, they actually had him in handcuffs on Monday, interviewed him at police headquarters and turned him loose, over the protest of many professionals who insisted the evidence was *there* to make an arrest for probable cause, just as they would have done for an ordinary person.

"He would have been in the can so Goddam fast it would have made your head spin," said public defender Jeff Brown in San Francisco, when asked how he would have handled the case, based upon what was known at the time. Daryl Gates, the controversial former police chief, ousted following the Los Angeles riots, said O.J. should have been picked up much earlier. "You can blame the District Attorney a little bit and you can blame the Police Department a lot," he observed with bitter irony, considering the department's abysmal record in the last years of his own administration.

The erroneous report about the bloody ski mask and the unexpected release of transcripts and recordings of some 911 emergency number calls made by Nicole Simpson had caused D.A. Garcetti heartburn. He wanted to button up the evidence and stop the leaks, to save it for the trial. Giving away information like that does nothing but aid the defense without making them work for it. After all, his job is to convict a charming, articulate, and beloved sports hero and

TV and movie star accused of butchering two people.

With O.J. safely behind bars, Garcetti could bounce back strongly from the black eye of the escape and refocus public opinion on the two victims, not on the alleged perpetrator. He went on a half-dozen nationally televised shows, gave newspaper interviews, and appeared in local TV spots to paint himself as outraged over the lenient sentence O.J. received in the wife-beating case, thus making himself a champion of the domestic abuse issue, while sidestepping questions about the pokey prosecutors who dawdled so long that Simpson had been given a golden opportunity to break free. He denied that O.J. had been given any special treatment.

There was no sign that Simpson was going to roll over on this one, and with Shapiro, a team of crackerjack specialists (soon to include such high-profile legal lights as F. Lee Bailey, counsel for Patty Hearst, and Alan and Nathan Dershowitz, whose clients included Klaus von Bulow, Leona Helmsley, and Mike Tyson), and a fortune to spend on the defense, the prosecution had its work cut out for them. Particularly with memories in their heads of how they blew the Menendez brothers' trial, even with a confession from the defendants. O.J. had said all along he didn't do it, had protested that he was innocent, even in what was thought to be his suicide note, and when he finally was arraigned in Los Angeles Municipal Court, he entered a plea of "Not guilty" to all charges.

The legal jockeying, sure to last months, began immediately, with Garcetti insisting he had a solid case against O.J. "It's not going to shock me if we see an O.J. Simpson, sometime down the road . . . say, 'O.K., I did do it, but I'm not responsible.' We've seen it in Menendez, and it's going to be a likely defense here," Garcetti speculated. Shapiro said, "Every possible defense has to be considered by a trial lawyer, and I certainly would reserve all possibilities."

If it is possible for anything good to emerge from this bloody tale, it is that the tragedy turned a spotlight on the problem of domestic abuse. Some four million women gave birth in the United States last year, and about an equal number were victims of domestic violence, including 1,432 who were murdered in such situations. Now the topic has moved to the front burner, demanding attention.

Garcetti and prosecutors raged at the

light sentence O.J. received in the 1989 beating incident, and the judge stepped forth to claim he had only followed the guidelines of the city attorney's office. Whoever was at fault, they allowed O.J. to brush off the incident as a mere embarrassment. It didn't teach him a thing, and apparently didn't deter him from continuing that violent pattern of behavior.

The California State Assembly, within days of the murders, expedited a resolution by a 42–8 vote that would require judges to attend a one-day session annually to receive domestic violence training. "The judge was not familiar with domestic violence. He felt it was a family matter," declared the resolution's sponsor, Bob Epple of Cerritos.

Black America is torn. A man who inspired them has been toppled, apparently of his own doing. Some say that O.J. was a role model, and others argue that a man who beats his wife should be despised, not idolized.

The lives of two innocent children have been forever altered. Thankfully, they have strong family members left to support them. Growing up should have been a joyful adventure for the kids of O.J. and Nicole. Instead, they probably will be plagued by unanswerable questions throughout their lives, and have nightmares of the brutal murder of their mother while they lay sleeping.

In the opinion of the author, Al Cowlings should be given a pass and a vote of thanks by the Los Angeles law people. He accomplished what the entire police apparatus, a high-priced attorney, other friends and professional people, and a mountain of media people failed to do. O.J.'s oldest pal not only stood by his friend at the darkest of moments, but he cajoled, wheedled, and persuaded O.J. *not* to carry out his very real suicide threat. When all was said and done, it was A.C. who delivered the distraught Simpson to justice. Alive. Unfortunately, the embarrassment of the escape left the establishment with a black eye, and looking for a scapegoat. Cowlings may be the fall guy. All of that could have been avoided if police had arrested Simpson earlier or assigned officers to watch the house where the celebrity suspect, whom they apparently knew they were going to charge, was staying. O.J.'s final run need never have occurred.

* * *

Perhaps this tells us something about how we choose our heroes. Just because someone is accomplished in sports or acting or politics, or any other public arena, does not mean they should be held up as a moral yardstick for our children. When a hero falls, the crash shakes the ground on which we all stand. The toppling of O.J. Simpson shook our spirit as well.

Appendix

I

Transcripts of Two 911 Calls Made by Nicole Simpson to Police on October 25, 1993

Nicole: Can you send someone to my house?

Dispatcher: What's the problem there?

Nicole: My ex-husband, or my husband, just broke into my house, and he's ranting and raving outside in the front yard.

Dispatcher: Has he been drinking or anything?

Nicole: No, but he's crazy.

Dispatcher: Did he hit you?

Nicole: No.

Dispatcher: Do you have a restraining order against him?

Nicole: No.

Dispatcher: What is your name?

Nicole: Nicole Simpson.

Dispatcher puts out a domestic violence call for any patrol car to respond to her address in Brentwood. About 50 seconds later, Nicole Simpson called back:

Nicole: Could you get somebody over here now, to . . . Gretna Green. He's back. Please.

Dispatcher: What does he look like?

Nicole: He's O.J. Simpson. I think you know his record. Could you just send somebody over here?

Dispatcher: What is he doing there?

Nicole: He just drove up again. [She begins to cry.] Could you just send somebody over?

Dispatcher: What is he driving?

Nicole: He's in a white Bronco, but first of all he broke the back door down to get in.

Dispatcher: Wait a minute, what's your name?

Nicole: Nicole Simpson.

Dispatcher: Okay. Is he the sportscaster or whatever?

Nicole: Yeah.

Dispatcher: Wait a minute, we're sending police. What is he doing? Is he threatening you?

Nicole: He's _____ [expletive deleted] going nuts [sobs].

Dispatcher: Has he threatened you, or is he just harassing you?

Nicole: You're going to hear him in a minute. He's about to come in again.

Dispatcher: Okay, just stay on the line.

Nicole: I don't want to stay on the line. He's going to beat the ____ [expletive deleted] out of me.

Dispatcher: Wait a minute, just stay on the line so we can know what's going on until the police get there, okay? Okay, Nicole?

Nicole: Uh-huh.

Dispatcher: Just a moment. Does he have any weapons?

Nicole: I don't know [exasperated]. He went home. Now he's back. The kids are up there sleeping and I don't want anything to happen.

Dispatcher: Okay, just a minute, is he on drugs or anything?

Nicole: No.

Dispatcher: Just stay on the line in case he comes in. I need to hear what's going on.

Nicole: Can you hear him outside?

Dispatcher: Is he yelling?

Nicole: Yep.

Dispatcher: Okay. Has he been drinking?

Nicole: No.

Dispatcher: Okay. [Speaking over radio to police units] . . . All units: More on the domestic violence at . . . South Gretna Green Way. The suspect has returned in a white Bronco. Monitor comments. Incident 48231.

Dispatcher: Okay, Nicole?

Nicole: Uh-huh.

Dispatcher: Is he outdoors?

Nicole: Uh-huh, he's in the back yard.

Dispatcher: He's in the back yard?

Nicole: Screaming at my roommate about me and at me.

Dispatcher: Okay. What is he saying?

Nicole: Oh, something about some guy I know and hookers and keys and I started this ____ [expletive deleted] before and . . .

Dispatcher: Um-hum.

Nicole: And it's all my fault and now what am I going to do, get the police in this? and the whole thing. It's all my fault. I started this before. [sigh] brother. [inaudible] kids [inaudible].

Dispatcher: Okay, has he hit you today or . . .

Nicole: No.

Dispatcher: Okay, you don't need any paramedics or anything?

Nicole: Uh-uh.

Dispatcher: Okay, you just want him to leave?

Nicole: My door. He broke the whole back door in.

Dispatcher: And then he left and came back?

Nicole: He came and he practically knocked my upstairs door down, but he pounded it and he screamed and hollered, and I tried to get him out of the bedroom because the kids are sleeping in there.

Dispatcher: Um-hum, okay.

Nicole: He wanted somebody's phone number and I gave him my phone book or I put my phone book down to write down the phone number that he wanted, and he took my phone book with all my stuff in it.

Dispatcher: Okay, so basically you guys have just been arguing?

[Simpson continues yelling inaudibly.]

Dispatcher: Is he inside right now?

Nicole: Yeah.

[O.J. still yelling]

Dispatcher: Okay, just a moment.

[More inaudible yelling by Simpson.]

Dispatcher: Is he talking to you?

Nicole: Yeah.

Dispatcher: Are you locked in a room or something?

Nicole: No. He can come right in. I'm not going where the kids are because the kids . . .

Dispatcher: Do you think he's going to hit you?

Nicole: I don't know.

Dispatcher: Stay on the line. Don't hang it up, okay?

Nicole: Okay.

[Inaudible.]

Dispatcher: What is he saying?
Nicole: What?
Dispatcher: What is he saying?
Nicole: What else.
[Sound of police radio traffic.]
Nicole: O.J., O.J., the kids are sleeping.
[More yelling.]
Dispatcher: He's still yelling at you?
[Sound of yelling. Nicole sobbing into telephone.]
Dispatcher: Is he upset with something that you did?
Nicole: [Sobs] A long time ago. It always comes back.
Dispatcher: Is your roommate talking to him?
Nicole: No one can talk, listen to him.
Dispatcher: Does he have any weapons with him right now?
Nicole: No, uh-uh.
Dispatcher: Okay. Where is he standing?
Nicole: In the back doorway, in the house.
Dispatcher: Okay.
O.J.: I don't give a ____ anymore . . . [expletive deleted].
Nicole: Would you just please, O.J. O.J., O.J., could you please [inaudible] Please leave.
O.J.: . . . I'm not leaving . . .

Nicole: Please leave. O.J., please, the kids, the kids are sleeping, please.

Dispatcher: Is he leaving?

Nicole: No.

Dispatcher: Does he know you're on the phone with police?

Nicole: No.

Dispatcher: Where are the kids at right now?

Nicole: Up in my room.

Dispatcher: Can they hear him yelling?

Nicole: I don't know. The room's the only one that's quiet . . . god.

Dispatcher: Is there someone up there with the kids?

Nicole: No.

[Yelling continues in the background.]

Dispatcher: What's he saying now? Nicole, you still on the line?

Nicole: Yeah.

Dispatcher: Do you still think he's going to hit you?

Nicole: I don't know. He's going to leave. He just said that. He just said he needs to leave.

O.J.: . . . Hey! I can read this bullshit all week in the *National Enquirer*. Her words exactly. What, who got that, who?

Dispatcher: Are you the only one in there with him?

Nicole: Right now, yeah. And he's also talking to my, the guy who lives out back is just standing there. He came home.

Dispatcher: Are you arguing with him, too?

Nicole: No! Absolutely not!

Dispatcher: Oh, okay, okay.

Nicole: That's not arguing.

Dispatcher: Yeah. Has this happened before or no?

Nicole: Many times.

Dispatcher: Okay. The police should be on the way. It just seems like a long time because it's kind of busy in that division right now.

[Yelling continues.]

Dispatcher, to police: Regarding Gretna Green Way, the suspect is still there and yelling very loudly.

Police officer on radio: 52 on Gretna Green.

Dispatcher: Is he still arguing?

[Knock at the door.]

Dispatcher: Was someone knocking on your door?

Nicole: It was him.

Dispatcher: He's knocking on your door?

Nicole: There's a locked bedroom and he's wondering why.

Dispatcher: Oh, so he's knocking on the locked door?

Nicole: Yeah. You know what, O.J.? That window above you is also open. Could you just go, please? Can I get off the phone?

Dispatcher: You want, you feel safe hanging up?

Nicole: [inaudible.]

Dispatcher: You want to wait till the police get there?

Nicole: Yeah.

Dispatcher: Nicole?

Nicole: Yeah.

Dispatcher: Is he still arguing with you?

Nicole: Um-hum. He's moved a little [inaudible].

Dispatcher: But the kids are still asleep?

Nicole: Yes. They're like rocks.

Dispatcher: What part of the house is he in right now?

Nicole: Downstairs.

Dispatcher: Downstairs?

Nicole: Yes.

Dispatcher: And you're upstairs?

Nicole: No, I'm downstairs in the kitchen . . . in the kitchen.

[Yelling continues in the background.]

Dispatcher: Can you see the police, Nicole?

Nicole: No, but I will go out there right now.

Dispatcher: Okay, you want to go out there?

Nicole: Yeah.

Dispatcher: Okay, hang up. Okay.

The police report stated O.J. Simpson admitted breaking in. But in a follow-up investigation, Nicole refused to prosecute and maintained the only reason the report was taken was because she was pressured by the police.

II

O.J. Simpson's
Professional Career Record

Year	Att.	Yards	Avg.	Long	TD
1969	181	697	3.9	32t*	2
1970	120	488	4.1	56t	5
1971	183	742	4.1	46t	5
1972	292	1,251	4.3	94t	6
1973	332	2,003	6.0	80t	12
1974	270	1,125	4.2	41t	3
1975	329	1,817	5.5	88t	16
1976	290	1,503	5.2	75t	8
1977	126	557	4.4	39	0
1978	161	593	3.7	34	1
1979	120	460	3.8	22	3
Career	2,404	11,236	4.7	94	61

* "t" denotes touchdown

RECEIVING
203 catches, 2,412 yards, 10.6 Avg., 64 long, 14 TD

KICKOFF RETURNS
33 carries, 990 yards, 30.0 Avg., 95 long, 1 TD

SCORING
76 TD, 456 points

III

Major Football Achievements

Heisman Trophy Winner
Number 1 draft pick, 1969
Unanimous All-Pro, 1972–1976
  1969 AFL All-Star Game
  Five Pro Bowls
  1973 Pro Bowl MVP
United Press International American Football
  Conference Player of the Year, 1972, 1973, 1974
Bert Bell Trophy Winner as Most Valuable Player in
  the National Football league, 1973
Four NFL Rushing titles
First player to rush for more than 2,000 yards in
  one season
Five 1,000 yard rushing seasons
14,368 combined net yards
Enshrined Hall of Fame 1985

1969   Buffalo Bills (AFL)
1970–1977   Buffalo Bills (NFL)
1978–1979   San Francisco 49ers

IV
Domestic Violence Hotlines and Shelters

Fourteen hundred women die each year in the U.S. as a result of domestic violence. If you, or someone you know, is trapped in an environment of abuse, help is available. While there is currently no national spousal abuse hotline, coalitions in all 50 states (and Puerto Rico) can provide information concerning domestic violence hotlines and shelters. Please don't wait—call today.

N.O.V.A. (National Organization for Victim Assistance) is a 24-hour information and referral service for victims of crime, including domestic violence. Their phone number is:
1-800/TRY-NOVA
1-800/879-6682

State Coalitions

ALABAMA:
Carol Gundlach
Alabama Coalition Against
Domestic Violence
PO Box 4762
Montgomery, AL 36101
PHONE: 205/832-4842
FAX: 205/832-4803

ALASKA:
Cindy Smith
Alaska Network on Domestic
Violence and Sexual
Assault
130 Seward Street, Suite 501
Juneau, AK 99801
PHONE: 907/586-3650
FAX: 907/463-4493

ARIZONA:
Sharon Ersch
Arizona Coalition Against
Domestic Violence
100 W. Camelback #109
Phoenix, AZ 85013
PHONE: 602/279-2900 or
FAX: 602/279-2980 (call
              first)

ARKANSAS:
Schatzi Riley
Arkansas Coalition Against
Violence to Women and
Children
7509 Cantrell Road, Ste 213
Little Rock, AR 72207
PHONE: 501/663-4668
FAX: 501/833-6646

CALIFORNIA:
Donna Garske
California Alliance Against
Domestic Violence
1717 5th Avenue
San Rafael, CA 94901
PHONE: 415/457-2464
FAX: 415/457-6457

COLORADO:
Jan Mickish
Colorado Coalition Against
Domestic Violence
PO Box 18902
Denver, CO 80218
PHONE: 309/573-9018
FAX: 307/573-9023

CONNECTICUT:
Sylvia Gafford-Alexander
Connecticut Coalition
Against Domestic Violence
135 Broad Street
Hartford, CT 06105
PHONE: 203/524-5890
FAX: 203/249-1408

DELAWARE:
Mary Davis
Delaware Domestic Violence
Task Force
c/o Child, Inc.,
507 Philadelphia Pike
Wilmington, DE 19809-2177
PHONE: 302/762-6110
FAX: 302/762-8983

DISTRICT OF COLUMBIA:
Donna Edwards
DC Coalition Against
Domestic Violence

252

PO Box 75069
Washington, DC 20013
PHONE: 202/543-0773
FAX: 202/543–2591 (call first)

FLORIDA:
Lucy Mohs
Florida Coalition Against
  Domestic Violence
PO Box 1201
Winter Park, FL 32790-1201
PHONE: N/A
FAX: N/A

Rita DeYoung
Hubbard House
PO Box 4909
Jacksonville, FL 32201
PHONE: 904/354-3122
FAX: 904/354-4034

GEORGIA:
Suzannah Pogue
Georgia Advocates for
  Battered Women and
  Children
250 Georgia Ave SE, Suite
  308
Atlanta, GA 30312
PHONE: 404/524-3847
FAX: 404/584-5803 (call first)

HAWAII:
Carol Lee
Hawaii State Committee on
  Family Violence
2500 Pali Highway
Honolulu, HI 96817-1455
PHONE: 808/595-6803
FAX: 808/532-3804

IDAHO:
Rose Moore
Idaho Network to Stop
  Violence Against Women
PO Box 714
Blackfoot, ID 83221
PHONE: 208/785-1047
FAX: N/A

ILLINOIS:
Vickie Smith
Illinois Coalition Against
  Domestic Violence
937 South Fourth Street
Springfield, IL 62703
PHONE: 217/789-2830
FAX: 217/789-1939

INDIANA:
Laura Berry
Indiana Coalition Against
  Domestic Violence
622 West 10th Street
Anderson, IN 46016
PHONE: 317/641-1912
FAX: 317/641-1912

IOWA:
Laurie Schipper
Iowa Coalition Against
  Domestic Violence
Lucas Building, First Floor
Des Moines, IA 50319
PHONE: 515/281-7284
FAX: 515/242-6119

KANSAS:
Trish Bledsoe
Kansas Coalition Against
  Sexual and Domestic
  Violence

820 SE Quincy Street,
#416B
Topeka, KS 66612-1158
PHONE: 913/232-9784
FAX: 913/232-9784, *51

KENTUCKY:
Sharon Allen Currens
Kentucky Domestic
  Violence Assoc.
PO Box 356
Frankfort, KY 40602
PHONE: 502/875-4132
FAX: 502/875-4268

Leslie Hamelman
Indiana Coalition Against
  Domestic Violence
PO Box 2048
Louisville, KY 40201
PHONE: 502/581-7231
FAX: 502/581-7204

LOUISIANA:
Patsy Taylor
Louisiana Coalition Against
  Domestic Violence
PO Box 3053
Hammond, LA 70404
PHONE: 504/542-4446
FAX: 504/542-7661

MAINE:
Tracy Cooley
Maine Coalition for Family
  Crisis Services
PO Box 89
Winterport, ME 04496
PHONE: 207/941-1194
FAX: N/A

MARYLAND:
Susan Mize
Maryland Network Against
  Domestic Violence
11501 Georgia Avenue, #403
Silver Spring, MD 20902
PHONE: 301/942-0900
FAX: 301/929-2589

MASSACHUSETTS:
Carolyn Ramsey or John
  Stiles
Massachusetts Coalition of
  Battered Women's Service
  Groups
210 Commercial Street, 3rd
floor
Boston, MA 02109
PHONE: 617/248-0922
FAX: 617/248-0902

Mercedes Tompkins
Massachusetts Coalition of
  Battered Women's Service
  Groups
14 Alpha Road
Dorchester, MA 02124
PHONE: 617/436-2122
FAX: N/A

MICHIGAN:
Joan Dauphine
Michigan Coaolition Against
  Domestic Violence
PO Box 16009
Lansing, MI 48901
PHONE: 517/484-2924
FAX: N/A

MINNESOTA:
Marsha Frey
Minnesota Coalition for
  Battered Women

1619 Dayton Avenue, Suite
303
St. Paul, MN 55104
PHONE: 612/646-6177
FAX: 612/646-1527

MISSISSIPPI:
Jane Philo
Mississippi Coalition
  Against Domestic Violence
PO Box 333
Biloxi, MS 39533
PHONE: 601/435-1968
FAX: 601/435-0513

MISSOURI:
Colleen Coble
Missouri Coalition Against
  Domestic Violence
331 Madison
Jefferson City, MO 65101
PHONE: 314/634-4161
FAX: 314/636-3728

MONTANA:
Jacqui Garcia
Montana Coalition Against
  Domestic Violence
1236 N. 28th Street, Suite
103
Billings, MT 59101-0114
PHONE: 406/245-7990
FAX: 406/252-1092

NEBRASKA:
Sarah O'Shea
Nebraska Domestic Violence
  & Sexual Assault Coalition
315 South 9th, Suite 18
Lincoln, NE 68508
PHONE: 402/476-6256
FAX: 402/477-0837

NEVADA:

Sue Meuschke
Nevada Network Against
  Domestic Violence
2100 Capurro Way,
  Suite 21-1
Sparks, NV 89431
PHONE: 702/358-1171
FAX: 702/358-0616

NEW HAMPSHIRE:
Susan L. Steiger
New Hampshire Coalition
  Against Domestic and
  Sexual Violence
PO Box 353
Concord, NH 03302-0353
PHONE: 603/224-8893 or
FAX: 603/226-1831

NEW JERSEY:
Barbara Price
New Jersey Coalition for
  Battered Women
2620 Whitehorse Hamilton
  Square Road
Trenton, NJ 08690-2718
PHONE: 609/584-8107
FAX: 609/584-9750

NEW MEXICO:
Marian Copas
New Mexico State Coalition
  Against Domestic Violence
2329 Wisconsin NE, Suite F
Albuquerque, NM 87110
PHONE: 505/296-7876
FAX: 505/292-3738

NEW YORK:
Sherry Frohman
New York State Coalition
  Against Domestic Violence

255

Women's Building,
79 Central Avenue
Albany, NY 12206
PHONE: 518/432-4864
FAX: 518/432-4864

NORTH CAROLINA:
Kathy Hodges
North Carolina Coalition
  Against Domestic Violence
PO Box 51875
Durham, NC 27717-1875
PHONE: 919/956-9124
FAX: 919/682-4629

NORTH DAKOTA:
Bonnie Palacek
North Dakota Council on
  Abused Women's Services
418 East Rosser Avenue,
  Suite 320
Bismarck, ND 58501
PHONE: 701/255-6240 or
FAX: 701/255-2411

OHIO:
Portia Gonzalez-McDade
Action Ohio Coalition for
  Battered Women
PO Box 15673
Columbus, OH 43215
PHONE: 614/221-1255
FAX: N/A

Daryl Kross
Ohio Domestic Violence
  Network
4041 North High Street
Columbus, OH 43214
PHONE: 614/784-0023
FAX: 614/784-0033

OKLAHOMA:

Georgie Rasco
Oklahoma Coalition on
  Domestic Violence and
  Sexual Assault
2200 Classen Boulevard,
  Suite 1300
Oklahoma City, OK 73106
PHONE: 405/557-1210
FAX: 405/557-1296

OREGON:
Pat Dirr
Oregon Coalition Against
  Domestic Violence
2336 SE Belmont Street
Portland, OR 97214
PHONE: 503/239-4486/ 4487
FAX: 503/233-9373

PENNSYLVANIA:
Susan Kelly-Dreiss
Pennsylvania Coalition
  Against Domestic Violence
6400 Flank Drive
Gateway Corp Center, #1300
Harrisburg, PA 17112
PHONE: 717/545-6400 or
FAX: 717/545-9456

PUERTO RICO:
Judith Spindt
Puerto Rico Coalition
  Against Domestic Violence
N-11 Calle 11, San Souci
Bayamón, PR 00619
PHONE: 809/722-2857
FAX: N/A

RHODE ISLAND:
Mary Trinity
Rhode Island Council on
  Domestic Violence
324 Broad Street

Central Falls, RI 02863
PHONE: 401/723-3051
FAX: 401/723-9643

SOUTH CAROLINA:
Ann Beckham
South Carolina Coalition
  Against Domestic Violence
  and Sexual Assault
PO Box 7776
Columbia, SC 29202-7776
PHONE: 803/254-3699
FAX: 803/425-4211

SOUTH DAKOTA:
Brenda Hill
South Dakota Coalition
  Against Domestic Violence
  and Sexual Assault
PO Box 689
Agency Village, SD 57262
PHONE: 605/698-3947
FAX: 605/698-3129

TENNESSEE:
Kathy England
Tennessee Task Force of
  Family Violence
PO Box 120972
Nashille, TN 37212-0972
PHONE: 615/327-0805
FAX: 615/321-9066

TEXAS:
Debby Tucker
Texas Council on Family
  Violence
8701 N. Mopac Expressway,
  Suite 450
Austin, TX 78759
PHONE: 512/794-1133
FAX: 512/794-1199

UTAH:

Diane Stuart
Citizens Against Physical
  and Sexual Abuse
PO Box 3617
Logan, UT 84321-3617
PHONE: 801/752-4493
FAX: 801/753-0372

VERMONT:
Judy Rex
Vermont Network Against
  Domestic Violence and
  Sexual Assault
PO Box 405
Montpelier, VT 05601
PHONE: 802/223-1902
FAX: 802/223-3751

VIRGINIA:
Ruth Micklem
Virginians Against
  Domestic Violence
2850 Sandy Bay Road,
  Suite 101
Williamsburg, VA 23185
PHONE: 804/221-0990
FAX: 804/229-1553

Nancy Turner
1706 DeWitt Avenue, Apt. H
Alexandria, VA 22301
PHONE: 703/765-0339
FAX: 703/765-0339

WASHINGTON:
Mary Pontarolo
Washington State Domestic
  Violence Hotline
200 W Street, SE, Suite B
Turnwater, WA 98501
PHONE: 206/352-4029
FAX: 206/352-4078

WEST VIRGINIA:

Sue Julian
West Virginia Coalition
  Against Domestic Violence
PO Box 85
307 Main Street
Sutton, WV 26601
PHONE: 304/765-2250
FAX: 304/765-2250

WISCONSIN:
Kathleen Krenek
Wisconsin Coalition Against
  Domestic Violence
1400 West Washington
  Avenue, S-103

Madison, WI 53703
PHONE: 608/255-0539
FAX: 608/284-2136

WYOMING:
Rosemary Bratton
Wyoming Coalition Against
  Domestic and Sexual
  Assault
341 East E Street, Suite
  135A
Casper, WY 82601
PHONE: 307/235-2814
FAX: 307/265-3609 (call
          first)